Behold the Pierced One

JOSEPH CARDINAL RATZINGER

Behold
The Pierced One

An Approach to a
Spiritual Christology

Translated by
GRAHAM HARRISON

IGNATIUS PRESS   SAN FRANCISCO

Title of the German original:
Schauen auf den Durchbohrten
© 1984 Johannes Verlag, Einsiedeln

Cover art: *The Incredulity of Saint Thomas*
A relief from a column at
the Abbey of Santo Domingo de Silos
in Northern Spain
© The Art Archive/Corbis

Cover design by Roxanne Mei Lum

With ecclesiastical approval
© 1986 Ignatius Press, San Francisco
ISBN 978-0-89870-087-9
Library of Congress catalogue number 86-80103
Printed in the United States of America ∞

This book is dedicated with gratitude to
FR. ALOIS GRILLMEIER
the great scholar of Christology

Contents

Preface

This little collection of christological meditations and reflections has two points of origin. The first was the Congress on the Sacred Heart of Jesus that was held at Toulouse in the summer of 1981 in connection with the Eucharistic Congress held earlier at Lourdes. In the quiet of the Dominican cloister in Toulouse I was able to work on my talk for the Congress, which became an impetus for me to consider Christology more from the aspect of its spiritual appropriation than I had previously done. During the same year I was unexpectedly led in the same direction by a very different event. The 1600-year commemoration of the First Ecumenical Council of Constantinople was being celebrated, as was the 1550-year anniversary of Ephesus; but, to my surprise, almost no attention was paid to the fact that the date of the Third Council of Constantinople—681— might also have been the occasion for a memorial. This caused me to acquaint myself more closely with the pronouncements of this Council. As I read the texts it became clear, much to my astonishment, that the achievement of a spiritual Christology had also been the Council's ultimate goal, and that it was only from this point of view that the classical formulas of Chalcedon appear in the proper perspective. I had no time to make a study of this particular theme, but the thought of a spiritual Christology remained with me and found its way into other works. It is from this perspective that the individual pieces were collected into this book, which, I admit, is more the presentation of a theme than its exposition. My heartfelt gratitude is due to Hans Urs von Balthasar, who, in connection with the Congress on the Sacred Heart of Jesus, encouraged me both patiently and persistently to attempt such a collection.

Joseph Cardinal Ratzinger
Rome, September 17, 1983

Part One

The Theological Basis
For a Spiritual Christology

Taking Bearings in Christology

Since the end of the Council the panorama of theology has changed fundamentally, not only as regards the matters debated by theologians, but also and in particular as regards the structure of theology itself. For whereas, prior to the Council, theological debate took place within a closely knit and uncontested framework, now the fundamentals themselves are widely matters of dispute. This is very evident in the case of Christology. Whereas, previously, discussion had centered on the various theories seeking to shed light on the hypostatic union or on particular questions such as Christ's knowledge, now people are asking, "How is the christological dogma related to the testimony of Scripture?" and "What is the relationship between biblical Christology, in its several phases of development, and the figure of the

This address was given in Rio de Janeiro in September 1982 at a congress on Christology organized by CELAM. Several of the addresses on that occasion analyzed particular and currently burning issues in Christology, whereas my task and aim was to present in some way the inner totality and unity, as it were, of Christology. For the loss of such a total view is the real central problem of the contemporary christological debate, and it cannot be met except by renewed attempts to embrace this totality, even if, at every step, questions of detail—which, in the compass of this book, cannot be dealt with thoroughly—threaten to ensnare us. I felt justified, because of the special nature of the project, in referring back more than usual to earlier publications of mine on the subject. I hope, all the same, that the reader will see that I am not simply reproducing earlier ideas but developing them in a new context which lends new significance to them.

real historical Jesus?"; "To what extent is the Church an expression of the will of Jesus?" In this connection it is significant that, in contemporary writing, the title "Christ" has largely given way to the personal name "Jesus". This linguistic change reveals a spiritual process with wide implications, namely, the attempt to get behind the Church's confession of faith and reach the purely historical figure of Jesus. He is no longer to be understood through this confession, but, as it were, in and through himself alone; and thus his achievement and his challenge are to be reinterpreted from scratch. Consequently people no longer speak of following Christ but of following Jesus: for "discipleship of Christ" implies the Church's confession that Jesus is the Christ, and hence it involves a basic acknowledgment of the Church as the primary form of discipleship. "Discipleship of Jesus", however, concentrates on the man Jesus who opposes all forms of authority; one of its features is a basically critical attitude to the Church, seen as a sign of its faithfulness to Jesus. This in turn goes beyond Christology and affects soteriology, which must necessarily undergo a similar transformation. Instead of "salvation" we find "liberation" taking pride of place, and the question, "How is the liberating act of Jesus to be mediated?" automatically adopts a critical stance over against the classical doctrine of how man becomes a partaker of grace.[1]

[1] On the contemporary christological debate, cf. Löhrer–Schütz–Wiederkehr (ed.), *Mysterium Salutis*, Supplement (Einsiedeln 1981), 220–50 (Wiederkehr); J. Pfammater–F. Furger (ed.), *Theologische Berichte II* (Einsiedeln 1973), esp. the article by D. Wiederkehr, 11–119; *Theologische Berichte VII* (1978); W. Beinert "Jesus—der vollkommene Mensch", in P. Gordan (ed.), *Menschwerden Menschsein* (Graz 1983), 371–424; L. F. Matero-Seco (ed.), *Cristo, Hijo de Dios y*

This indicates something of the task which today faces a theology which understands itself as interpreting the common faith of the Church, not as reconstructing a vanished Jesus, at long last piecing together his real history. It is impossible, within the present compass, to answer all the many questions that face us at this point. That will be the task for a whole generation at least. My intention is more modest, namely, to put forward in a few theses certain fundamental characteristics of the indivisible inner unity of Jesus and Christ, Church and history.

Thesis 1: According to the testimony of Holy Scripture, the center of the life and person of Jesus is his constant communication with the Father.

Let us try to develop this idea a little further. The developing Church—like the contemporaries of the earthly Jesus—saw herself presented with the question as to who this Jesus was, "Who is he?" (cf. Mk 8:27–30). The answers of the "people" in the time of Jesus, as reported in the Gospels, reflect the attempt to find, in the arsenal of the known and nameable, categories in which to describe the figure of Jesus. We see the same in Simon Peter's famous avowal, which has become part of the Church's confession. Although Peter's confession provided a fundamental orientation, regarded by believers

Redentor del Hombre (Pamplona 1982). Basic, still, are W. Kasper, *Jesus the Christ* (London 1976); L. Bouyer, *The Eternal Son* (Indiana 1978); H. U. von Balthasar, *Theodramatik II* and *III* (Einsiedeln 1978 and 1980). On the Protestant side, in addition to Pannenberg, *Jesus God and Man* (London 1968), cf. esp. H. Thielicke, *Gotteslehre und Christologie* (Tübingen 1973) and G. Ebeling, *Dogmatik des christl. Glaubens II* (Tübingen 1982).

as pointing in the right direction, the single formula, "Jesus is the Christ, the Messiah" was not sufficient by itself. In the first place the title "Messiah" had many different meanings; the argument between Jesus and Peter which concludes Peter's confession clearly shows the problems connected with the word (Mk 8:31–33). The way Peter's confession in Mark is developed in Luke and Matthew also clearly shows the need for explanation and clarification; what we have here is a piece of the Church's credal history within the synoptic tradition itself.

Thus we can say that, though this basic confession of faith provided the infant Church with a nucleus around which her interpretation of Jesus could crystallize, it also opened up a wide field of further interpretations, as is evident from the wealth of additional titles, e.g., Prophet, Priest, Paraclete, Angel, Lord, Son of God, Son. In concrete terms, the struggle to arrive at a proper understanding of Christ in the primitive Church is the struggle to sift these titles of Jesus and put them in the correct perspective and order. In short, the whole process can be described as one of increasing simplification and concentration. In the end only three titles remain as the community's valid adumbration of the mystery of Jesus: Christ, Lord and Son (of God).

Since the title Christ (Messiah) became more and more associated with the name Jesus and had little clear meaning outside a Jewish milieu; and since "Lord", too, was not as clear as "Son", a further concentration took place: the title "Son" comes in the end to be the only, comprehensive designation for Jesus. It both comprises and interprets everything else. So, finally, the Church's confession of faith can be satisfied with this title. We find it in its ultimate form in Matthew, in Peter's confession: "You are the Christ, the Son of the living God" (Mt 16:16). In bringing the many strands of tradition together in this one word and thus imparting an ultimate simplicity to the fundamental Christian option, the Church was not oversimplifying and reducing; in the word "Son" she had found that simplicity which is both profound and all-embracing. "Son" is a basic confession in the sense that it provides the key to interpretation, making everything else accessible and intelligible.[2]

At this point, however, we are obliged to turn to the question of origins. Modern exegesis and history of doctrine are in principle suspicious that this kind of concentration of the historical inheritance may be a falsification of the original phenomenon simply because the historical distance is too great. In fact, however, in concentrating on "Son" as the comprehensive interpretative category for the figure of Jesus, the Church was responding precisely to the basic historical experience of those who had been eyewitnesses of Jesus' life. Calling Jesus the "Son", far from overlaying him with the mythical gold of dogma (a view that has been put forward ever since Reimarus), corresponds most strictly to the center of the historical figure of Jesus. For the entire gospel testimony is unanimous that Jesus' words and deeds flowed from his most intimate communion with the Father; that he continually went "into the hills" to pray in solitude after the burden of the day (e.g., Mk 1:35; 6:46; 14:35, 39). Luke, of all the Evangelists, lays stress on this feature.[3] He shows that the essential events of Jesus' activity proceeded from the core of his person-

[2] Cf. J. Ratzinger, *Theologische Prinzipienlehre* (Munich 1982), 17–22; H. Schlier, "Die Anfänge des christologischen Credo", in B. Welte (ed.), *Zur Frühgeschichte der Christologie* (Freiburg 1970), 13–58.

[3] The following points develop ideas adumbrated in my book *Der Gott Jesu Christi* (Munich 1976), 66–68.

ality and that this core was his dialogue with the Father. Here are three examples:

1. Let us begin with the calling of the Twelve, a symbolic number indicating the new People of God, whose pillars they were destined to be. In them, therefore, in a gesture of Jesus which is both sign and reality, he inaugurates the "People of God" in a new way, i.e., their calling is to be seen theologically as the beginning of all that is "Church". According to Luke, Jesus had spent the night which preceded this event at prayer on the mountain: the calling of the Twelve proceeds from prayer, from the Son's converse with the Father. The Church is born in that prayer in which Jesus gives himself back into the Father's hands and the Father commits everything to the Son. This most profound communication of Son and Father conceals the Church's true and ever-new origin, which is also her firm foundation (Lk 6:12–17).

2. Next I cite the account of the very origin of the Christian confession of faith, which, as we have already mentioned, is the prime source for the earliest history of christological dogma. Jesus asks the disciples what men say of him and what they themselves think about him. As is well known, Peter replies with the confession which, then as now, is constitutive of the Church in fellowship with Peter. The Church lives by this confession, which unlocks both the mystery of Jesus and the mystery of human life, of human history and of the world, because it manifests the mystery of God. This confession unites the Church, which is why the Simon who makes it is called Peter, designated and appointed the rock of unity. Thus the confession and the Petrine office, the confession of faith in Jesus and the unity of the Church, are inseparably linked together with Peter and centered on him.

We can say, therefore, that Peter's confession represents the second stage of the Church's taking shape. Again it is Luke who shows that Jesus put the crucial question of how the disciples stood toward him at the very moment when they had begun to share in the hiddenness of his prayer. In this way the Evangelist makes it clear that Peter had grasped and expressed the most fundamental reality of the person of Jesus as a result of having seen him praying, in fellowship with the Father. According to Luke, we see who Jesus is if we see him at prayer. The Christian confession of faith comes from participating in the prayer of Jesus, from being drawn into his prayer and being privileged to behold it; it interprets the experience of Jesus' prayer, and its interpretation of Jesus is correct because it springs from a sharing in what is most personal and intimate to him.

Thus we have arrived at both the very basis and the abiding precondition of the Christian confession of faith: only by entering into Jesus' solitude, only by participating in what is most personal to him, his communication with the Father, can one see what this most personal reality is; only thus can one penetrate to his identity. This is the only way to understand him and to grasp what "following Jesus" means. The Christian confession is not a neutral proposition; it is prayer, only yielding its meaning within prayer. The person who has beheld Jesus' intimacy with his Father and has come to understand him from within is called to be a "rock" of the Church. The Church arises out of participation in the prayer of Jesus (cf. Lk 9:18–20; Mt 16:13–20).

3. My third example is the story of Jesus' Transfiguration "on the mountain".[4] In the Gospels, "the

[4] Cf. H. Schürmann, *Das Lukasevangelium I* (Freiburg 1969), 553–67; for important remarks on the interpretation of the Transfiguration story, cf. H. Gese, *Zur biblischen Theologie* (Munich 1977), 80f.

mountain" is always the realm of prayer, of being with the Father. It was to this "mountain" that Jesus had taken the Three who formed the core of the community of the Twelve: Peter, James and John. "As he was praying, the appearance of his countenance was altered", Luke tells us (9:29). Thus he makes it plain that the Transfiguration only renders visible what is actually taking place in Jesus' prayer: he is sharing in God's radiance and hence in the manner in which the true meaning of the Old Testament —and of all history—is being made visible, i.e., revelation. Jesus' proclamation proceeds from this participation in God's radiance, God's glory, which also involves a seeing with the eyes of God—and therefore the unfolding of what was hidden. So Luke also shows the unity of revelation and prayer in the person of Jesus: both are rooted in the mystery of Sonship. Furthermore, according to the Evangelists, the Transfiguration is a kind of anticipation of Resurrection and parousia (cf. Mk 9:1). For his communication with the Father, which becomes visible in his prayer in the Transfiguration, is the true reason why Jesus could not remain in death and why all history is in his hands. He whom the Father addresses is the Son (cf. Jn 10:33–36). But the Son cannot die. Thus Luke suggests that the whole of Christology—our speaking of Christ— is nothing other than the interpretation of his prayer: the entire person of Jesus is contained in his prayer.

4. Many other instances illustrating this view can be adduced from the other Evangelists. Again I would like briefly to mention just three of them.

a. My first is the prayer of Jesus on the Mount of Olives, which, now that the hour of his Passion has begun to strike, has become the mountain of his solitude with the Father. The "Abba" with which Jesus addresses God, which Mark has preserved for us in Jesus' Aramaic mother tongue, goes beyond every mode of prayer then known; it expresses a familiarity with God which would have appeared impossible and unseemly to the Jewish tradition. Thus this one, unique word expresses the new and unique manner of Jesus' relationship to God—a relationship which, on his own side, calls for the term "Son" as the only possible one.[5]

b. This brings us to my second point, which is the absolutely fundamental role played by the terms "Father" and "Son" in Jesus' vocabulary. Jesus never called the disciples or other people "son" or "sons" in the same way as himself. Furthermore, he used the expression "my Father" in a way which clearly distinguished it from the general Fatherhood of God which embraces all men. The "*Our* Father" form of address is intended for the disciples, who say "we" as they pray as a community; it expresses the fact that those who belong to Jesus participate in Jesus' relationship to God through their community prayer, without blurring the difference between their respective modes of relationship to God. In all the words and deeds of Jesus, this filial relationship always shines through, ever-present and ever-creative; we perceive that his whole being is at home in this relationship.

c. This relationship, this being of his, which fashions from within and which *is* the person of Jesus, is not only seen in the various forms of the word "Son": it also occurs in a series of formulas which are found throughout Jesus' preaching, e.g., "therefore have I come"; "therefore was I sent". In Jesus' own awareness, as we see it in the Gospels, he does not speak and act from himself but from Another: it is of his very essence that he comes

---

[5] J. Jeremias, *The Prayers of Jesus* (London 1967), chap. 1.

from this Other. His entire existence is a "sending", a "mission", i.e., a relationship.[6]

Once we have observed these features in the synoptic Gospels, it becomes clear that the Fourth Gospel, which is built wholly on concepts like "Word", "Son" and "send", adds nothing alien to the older tradition but only underscores what the other Gospels present to us. We could say that the Fourth Gospel draws us into that intimacy which Jesus reserved for those who were his friends. It shows Jesus from the experience of friendship which allows us to glimpse inner realities.

Thesis 2: Jesus died praying. At the Last Supper he had anticipated his death by giving of himself, thus transforming his death, from within, into an act of love, into a glorification of God.

After what we have reflected on in Thesis 1, this second thesis requires relatively little explanation. For in Jesus' prayer we have discovered the clue linking together Christology and soteriology, the person of Jesus and his deeds and sufferings. Although the Evangelists' accounts of the last words of Jesus differ in details, they agree on the fundamental fact that Jesus died praying. He fashioned his death into an act of prayer, an act of worship. According to Matthew and Mark he raised his voice to a "loud cry" as he uttered the opening words of Psalm 21, the great psalm of the suffering and yet rescued righteous man: "My God, my God, why hast thou forsaken me?" (Mk 15:34; Mt 27:46). Both Evangelists also tell us that these words were not understood by the bystanders, who interpreted Jesus' cry as his calling for Elijah. According to them, therefore, it needed faith to un-

[6] Valuable pointers in C. M. Martini, *Damit ihr Frieden habt. Geistliches Leben nach dem Johannesevangelium* (Freiburg 1982), 76f.

derstand that this death cry of Jesus was the messianic prayer of the great psalm of the sufferings and hopes of Israel, concluding with the prospect of the poor being satisfied and the ends of the earth being turned to the Lord. This psalm was a christological key-text for the earliest Christians; in it they found a prophecy, not only of Jesus' death on the Cross, but also of the mystery of the Eucharist stemming from the Cross, which truly satisfies the "poor", as well as of the Church of the Gentiles which likewise comes from the Cross. So this death cry, which was taken by those who witnessed it to be a vain call to Elijah for help, became, for Christians, the most profound interpretation of Jesus' death, which he himself had given it. The theology of the Cross found in this psalm applied to him just as much as the promise it held out; from the vantage point of the promise's fulfillment, this attribution was shown to be true; the psalm was shown to be Jesus' own word: no one else could pray it as truly as he could, rejected and despised, and yet, in this very condition, sustained and glorified by the Father. It must be borne in mind that the whole story of the Passion was woven, again and again, from the threads of this psalm; the account reveals a constant interpenetration of word and reality: here the archetypal suffering, portrayed anonymously by this psalm, had become concrete reality; here this primal suffering on the part of the Righteous One—apparently rejected by God—had actually taken place. Thus it became clear that Jesus was the true speaker of this psalm, that he had undergone that suffering from which came the feeding of the poor and the turning of the nations to worship the God of Israel.[7]

But let us return once more to our point of departure. As we saw, there was no unanimous tradition as to

[7] Cf. R. Pesch, *Das Markusevangelium II* (Freiburg 1977), 494ff. (with refs.).

precisely what were the last words of Jesus. Luke envisages them as coming, not from Psalm 21, but from the other great Passion psalm, 31 (v. 6, cf. Lk 23:46); John chooses a different verse (15) from Psalm 21 and links it with the Passion Psalm 68 (Jn 19:28f.). But the gospel tradition is unanimous about two things, and consequently every theological interpretation must concentrate upon them: common to all the Evangelists is the conviction that Psalm 21—in its entirety—was connected in a special way with the Passion of Jesus, with its actuality as well as with Jesus' acceptance of it.

Moreover, they all agree that the last words of Jesus were an expression of his devotion to his Father and that his cry was not uttered to anyone, anywhere, but to Him, since it was of his innermost essence to be in a dialogue relationship with the Father. Thus they all agree that his dying was itself an act of prayer, his death handing-over of himself to the Father. Finally they all agree that Jesus prayed in the words of Scripture and that Scripture became flesh in him, became the actual Passion of this Righteous One; and that he thus inserted his death into the word of God, in which he lived and which lived in him, declaring itself in him.

Once this has been seen, the indissoluble bond between the Supper and the death of Jesus is also plain: his dying words fuse with his words at the Supper, the reality of his death fuses with the reality of the Supper. For the event of the Supper consists in Jesus sharing his body and his blood, i.e., his earthly existence; he gives and communicates himself. In other words, the event of the Supper is an anticipation of death, the transformation of death into an act of love. Only in this context can we understand what John means by calling Jesus' death the glorification of God and the glorification of the Son (Jn

12:28; 17:21). Death, which, by its very nature, is the end, the destruction of every communication, is changed by him into an act of self-communication; and this is man's redemption, for it signifies the triumph of love over death. We can put the same thing another way: death, which puts an end to words and to meaning, itself becomes a word, becomes the place where meaning communicates itself.

Thesis 3: Since the center of the person of Jesus is prayer, it is essential to participate in his prayer if we are to know and understand him.

Let us begin here with a very general matter of epistemology. By nature, knowledge depends on a certain similarity between the knower and the known. The old axiom is that like is known by like. In matters of the mind and where persons are concerned, this means that knowledge calls for a certain degree of empathy, by which we enter, so to speak, into the person or intellectual reality concerned, become one with him or it, and thus become able to understand (*intellegere = ab intus legere*).

We can illustrate this with a couple of examples. Philosophy can only be acquired if we philosophize, if we carry through the process of philosophical thought; mathematics can only be appropriated if we think mathematically; medicine can only be learned in the practice of healing, never merely by means of books and reflection. Similarly, religion can only be understood through religion —an undisputed axiom in more recent philosophy of religion. The fundamental act of religion is prayer, which in the Christian religion acquires a very specific character: it is the act of self-surrender by which we enter the Body of Christ. Thus it is an act of love. As love, in and with the Body of Christ, it is always both love of God and love of neighbor, knowing and fulfilling itself as love for the members of this Body.

In Thesis 1 we saw that prayer was the central act of the person of Jesus and, indeed, that this person is constituted by the act of prayer, of unbroken communication with the one he calls "Father". If this is the case, it is only possible really to understand this person by entering into this act of prayer, by participating in it. This is suggested by Jesus' saying that no one can come to him unless the Father draws him (Jn 6:44). Where there is no Father, there is no Son. Where there is no relationship with God, there can be no understanding of him who, in his innermost self, is nothing but relationship with God, the Father—although one can doubtless establish plenty of details about him. Therefore a participation in the mind of Jesus, i.e., in his prayer, which (as we have seen) is an act of love, of self-giving and self-expropriation to men, is not some kind of pious supplement to reading the Gospels, adding nothing to knowledge of him or even being an obstacle to the rigorous purity of critical knowing. On the contrary, it is the basic precondition if real understanding, in the sense of modern hermeneutics—i.e., the entering-in to the same time and the same meaning—is to take place.

The New Testament continually reveals this state of affairs and thus provides the foundation for a theological epistemology. Here is simply one example: when Ananias was sent to Paul to receive him into the Church, he was reluctant and suspicious of Paul; the reason given to him was this: go to him "for he is praying" (Acts 9:11). In prayer, Paul is moving toward the moment when he will be freed from blindness and will begin to see, not only exteriorly, but interiorly as well. The person who prays begins to see; praying and seeing go together because— as Richard of St. Victor says—"Love is the faculty of seeing".[8] Real advances in Christology, therefore, can never come merely as the result of the theology of the schools, and that includes the modern theology as we find it in critical exegesis, in the history of doctrine and in an anthropology oriented toward the human sciences, etc. All this is important, as important as schools are. But it is insufficient. It must be complemented by the theology of the saints, which is theology from experience. All real progress in theological understanding has its origin in the eye of love and in its faculty of beholding.

Thesis 4: Sharing in Jesus' praying involves communion with all his brethren. Fellowship with the person of Jesus, which proceeds from participation in his prayer, thus constitutes that all-embracing fellowship that Paul calls the "Body of Christ". So the Church—the "Body of Christ"—is the true subject of our knowledge of Jesus. In the Church's memory the past is present because Christ is present and lives in her.

In teaching his disciples to pray, Jesus told them to say "*Our* Father" (Mt 6:9). No one but he can say "my Father". Everyone else is only entitled, as a member of the community, to use that "we" which Jesus made possible for them; i.e., they have the right to address God as Father because they are all created by God and for one another. To recognize and accept God's Fatherhood

[8] PL 196:1203. Cf. E. von Ivánka, *Plato Christianus* (Einsiedeln 1964), 333; on the whole context, 309–51.

always means accepting that we are set in relation to one another: man is entitled to call God "Father" to the extent that he participates in that "we"—which is the form under which God's love seeks for him.[9]

This connection corresponds to an insight on the part of human reason and historical experience. No one can build a bridge to the Infinite by his own strength. No one's voice is loud enough to summon the Infinite. No intelligence can adequately and securely conceive who God is, whether he hears us and how we should act toward him. As a result, in the entire history of religion and of the mind, we can observe a peculiar dichotomy in the question of God. On the one hand, there has always been a kind of basic evidence for the reality of God—and there still is. What Paul asserts in the Letter to the Romans, taking up a theme from the Old Testament Book of Wisdom (Wis 13:4), i.e., that the Creator can be seen in creation and is therefore evident (Rom 1:19f.), is by no means a dogmatic postulate but an observed fact which is confirmed by the history of religion. But Paul takes up and expands the idea of the Book of Wisdom by adding that this evidence goes hand in hand with a tremendous obscuring and twisting of the image of God. This too is a sober description of fact: the basic certainty of the existence of God was and is always accompanied by a sense of its being an immense riddle. Once we attempt to name and describe this God in more detail, once we try to relate human life to him and respond to him, the image of God falls apart in contradictory aspects. They do not simply eliminate the primary evidence, but they so obscure it as to make it unrecognizable; indeed, in extreme cases, they can actually destroy it entirely.[10]

[9] Cf. Cyprian, De dominica oratione 10–11, CSEL III 1:273f.

[10] Cf. the wealth of material in M. Eliade, A History of Religious Ideas (1979).

A consideration of the history of religion yields a further result: the theme of revelation crops up regularly. Negatively, this shows that man is not in a position to produce a relationship to God on his own account. He knows that he cannot compel the Divinity to enter into a relationship with him. Positively it means that the existing means of relating to God go back to an initiative on the latter's part, the tradition of which is passed on within a community as the wisdom of the ancients. To that extent, even the awareness that religion must rest on a higher authority than that of one's own reason, and that it needs a community as a "carrier", is part of mankind's basic knowledge, though found in manifold forms and even distortions.

At this juncture we can return to the figure of Jesus. Although Jesus stood in a very unique personal relationship to God, he did not simply depart from the basic pattern we have just described, with its essential features of community and revelation. He lived his religious life within the framework of the faith and tradition of God's People of Israel. His constant dialogue with the God of the Patriarchs, with his Father, was also a conversation with Moses and Elijah (cf. Mk 9:4). In this dialogue he passed beyond the letter of the Old Testament and laid bare its spirit in order to reveal the Father "in the Spirit". In doing so, however, he did not destroy the letter of the Old Testament, i.e., the common religious tradition of Israel, but showed its real depth for the first time, "fulfilled" it. Thus, too, this dialogue did not destroy the idea of the "People of God": it renewed it. Pulling down the wall of the letter resulted in giving the nations access to the Spirit of revelation and hence to God the Father, the God of Jesus Christ. This universalization of the tradition is its ultimate ratification, not its abrogation or replacement. If we grasp this, it becomes clear that

Jesus did not need to start by founding a People of God (the "Church"). It was already there. Jesus' task was only to renew this People by deepening its relationship to God and by opening it up for all mankind. Therefore the question of whether Jesus intended to found a Church is a false question because it is unhistorical. The only proper way to phrase the question would be to ask whether Jesus intended to abolish the People of God or to renew it. The answer to this question, rightly put, is plain: Jesus made the old People of God into a new People by adopting those who believe in him into the community of his own self (of his "Body"). He achieved this by transforming his death into an act of prayer, an act of love, and thus by making himself communicable. Put differently, Jesus has entered into the already existing subject of tradition, God's People of Israel, with his proclamation and his whole person, and by doing so he has made it possible for people to participate in his most intimate and personal act of being, i.e., his dialogue with the Father. That is the deepest layer of meaning of that process in which he taught his disciples to say "Our Father".

This being so, fellowship with Jesus and the resultant knowledge of Jesus presupposes that we are in communication with the living subject of tradition to which all this is linked—in communication with the Church. The message of Jesus has never been able to live and mediate life except in this communion. Even the New Testament, as a book, presupposes the Church as its subject.[11] It

[11] Cf. International Theological Commission, *Die Einheit des Glaubens und der theologische Pluralismus* (Einsiedeln 1973), 32–42. On the questions of exegesis and communication theory which underlie these remarks, cf. the important book by P. G. Müller, *Der Traditionsprozess im Neuen Testament* (Freiburg 1982).

grew in and from the Church; its unity comes solely from the Church's faith, which brings together diverse elements into a unity. We can see this mutual involvement of tradition, knowledge and community life in all the writings of the New Testament. In order to express it, the Gospel of John and the Johannine letters coined the "ecclesial we". Thus, for example, in the concluding verses of the first Letter of John, we come across the formula "we know" three times (5:1–20). It is also to be found in Jesus' conversation with Nicodemus (Jn 3:11); in each case it points to the Church as the subject of knowledge in faith.

The concept of "remembrance" in the Fourth Gospel plays a similar role. The Evangelist uses it to show the intertwining of tradition and knowledge. Most of all, however, he makes it clear how progress and the preservation of faith's identity mutually sustain one another. We could put it like this: the Church's tradition is the transcendental subject in whose memory the past is present. As a result of this, as time moves on, and in the light of the Holy Spirit who leads men to the truth (16:13; cf. 14:26), what is already present in the memory is seen more clearly and better understood. This advance is not the advent of something entirely new but the process whereby the memory becomes aware of itself.

This dependence of religious knowledge, knowledge of Jesus and God, on the Church's community remembrance by no means excludes the personal responsibility to exercise one's reason, nor does it hinder it. Rather, it provides the hermeneutical context for a rational understanding; i.e., it leads to the point where my "I" fuses with the "other" and hence to the realm of understanding. This remembrance on the part of the Church lives by being enriched and deepened by the experience of a love which worships; but it also lives by being continually refined by critical reason. The ecclesial quality of theology, which we have just outlined, is thus not an epistemological collectivism, not an ideology which violates reason, but a hermeneutical context which is essential to reason if it is to operate at all.[12]

Thesis 5: The core of the dogma defined in the councils of the early Church consists in the statement that Jesus is the true Son of God, of the same essence as the Father and, through the Incarnation, equally of the same essence as us. Ultimately this definition is nothing other than an interpretation of the life and death of Jesus, which was preordained from the Son's primal conversation with the Father. That is why dogmatic and biblical Christology cannot be divorced from one another or opposed to one another, no more than Christology and soteriology can be separated. In the same way, Christology "from above" and "from below", the theology of the Incarnation and the theology of the Cross, form an indivisible unity.

Having made these affirmations, let us turn back to Theses 1 and 2. If what we said there was a correct interpretation of the content of the biblical testimony,

[12] In the struggle against the ideological disintegration of theology caused by nazism, H. Schlier made a great contribution by maintaining the ecclesial nature of theology. Today, reading his lectures on the theology student's responsibility to the Church, and on the Church's responsibility for the teaching of theology, one is amazed at their contemporary relevance. They are reprinted in H. Schlier, *Der Geist und die Kirche* (Freiburg 1980), 225–50.

Thesis 5 follows automatically. The dogma's basic assertion, "the Son is of the same substance", which summarizes the entire witness of the ancient councils, simply puts the fact of Jesus' prayer into the technical language of philosophical theology, nothing more.

Certainly, this result is contradicted by the widespread view that Scripture and dogma arose in two different cultures: Scripture in the Hebrew culture, dogma in the Greek. It is said that putting the biblical testimony into the forms of Greek philosophical thought brought about a complete refashioning of what was once the plain witness to Jesus. Faith, which up to then had been a simple act of trust in saving grace, had become changed into an assent to philosophical paradoxes, to a belief in particular teachings. Thus, trust in God's action was supplanted by an ontological doctrine which is totally alien to Scripture.

Here we must interpose a very simple, basic human question. For the whole argument about Christ revolves around man's "liberation", his "salvation". But what can liberate man? Who liberates him, and to what? Put even more simply: What is "human freedom"? Can man become free without truth, i.e., in falsehood? Liberation without truth would be a lie; it would not be freedom but deception and thus man's enslavement, man's ruin. Freedom without truth cannot be true freedom, so, without truth, freedom is not even freedom.[13]

Let us take up another line of thought. If man is to be free, he must be "like God". Wanting to be like God is the inner motive of all mankind's programs of liberation. Since the yearning for freedom is rooted in man's being,

---

[13] On the various dimensions of the concept of freedom, especially the relationship of freedom and truth, cf. M. Kriele, *Befreiung und politische Aufklärung* (Freiburg 1980), esp. 83–103.

right from the outset he is trying to become "like God". Indeed, anything less is ultimately too little for him. We see this very clearly in our own time, with its passionate and strident demands for anarchic, total freedom, dissatisfied as it is with all the bourgeois freedoms and libertinisms, be they ever so great. If it is to do justice to its own aims, therefore, an anthropology of liberation will have to face the question: what is meant by "becoming like God", "becoming God"?

Now let us try to bring these two lines of thought into one focus. What do we see? When man poses the questions which are most vital to him, questions that are inescapable, i.e., about truth and freedom, he is asking ontological questions. The question of being, which is so slandered today, arose for no other reason than the desire for freedom, which cannot be divorced from man's need for truth. So it cannot be said that the question of being belongs only to a particular phase of mankind's intellectual development, to the age of metaphysics, which A. Comte, in accordance with his three-stage law, allots to the middle phase, between the mythical age and the positive age. (In Comte's view, we are now in the latter stage, in which the erstwhile metaphysical question is obsolete.)[14]

It is uncontested that the human sciences, which attempt to give a "positive" account of man in the sense of modern scientific methods, can yield important insights into man's nature. But they cannot render superfluous the question as to man's real truth, i.e., the question of from where this phenomenon of man comes and what is his destiny. If the human sciences were to try to make the question of truth superfluous, they would become tools

[14] On Comte: H. de Lubac, *The Drama of Atheist Humanism* (1949).

of self-alienation and hence of man's enslavement. The question of truth and the question of freedom are involved in the question of being and therefore also in the question of God. Indeed, they *are* the question of God. So, whereas it is certainly possible to allocate the methods of patristic theology to a particular time, and thus to indicate the limits of this theology, the questions which it has posed are always and everywhere necessary to man. An interpretation of the New Testament which puts these questions on one side is missing the essential point; it becomes a mere collection of marginalia.

This brings us back to our concrete question. At first sight it may seem to be a rather parochial, merely internal Christian matter, when we speak of the prayer of Jesus as the New Testament's basic affirmation regarding his person. In reality this is precisely the point which concerns us; i.e., it is what is central to humanity. For the New Testament designates it as the place where man may actually become God, where his liberation may take place; it is the place where he touches his own truth and becomes true himself. The question of Jesus' filial relation to the Father gets to the very root of the question of man's freedom and liberation, and unless this is done everything else is futile. Any liberation of man which does not enable him to become divine betrays man, betrays his boundless yearning.

Let us add an observation concerning the language of the dogma. At one point in its Creed, as is well known, the Council of Nicaea clearly went beyond the language of Scripture, in describing Jesus as "of one substance with the Father". Both in ancient and modern times the presence in the Creed of this philosophical term, "of one substance", has given rise to major disputes. Again and again it has been suggested that it indicates a serious departure not only from the language but also from the thought of the Bible. We can only answer this charge if we ascertain precisely what it actually says. What does "of one substance" really mean? The answer is this: the term is used solely as a translation of the word "Son" into philosophical language. And why is it necessary to translate it? Well, whenever faith begins to reflect, the question arises as to what, in reality, the word "Son" might mean as applied to Jesus. The word is very familiar in the language of the religions, and so people cannot avoid asking what it means in this particular case. Is it a metaphor, as is commonly found in the history of religion, or does it mean more? The Council of Nicaea, in interpreting the word "Son" philosophically by means of the concept "of one substance", is saying that "Son" is to be understood here, not in the sense of religious metaphor, but in the most real and concrete sense of the word. The central word of the New Testament, the word "Son", is to be understood literally.

So this philosophical phrase, "of one substance", adds nothing to the New Testament; on the contrary, at the crucial point of its testimony, it defends its literal meaning so that it cannot be allegorized. Thus it signifies that God's word does not deceive us. Jesus is not only *described* as the Son of God, he *is* the Son of God. God does not remain hidden for all eternity beneath the clouds of imagery which obscure more than they reveal. He actually touches man, and allows himself to be touched by man, in the person of him who *is* the Son. In speaking of the Son, the New Testament breaks through the wall of imagery found in the history of religions and shows us the reality—the truth on which we can stand, by which we can live and die. Thus we can say that it is precisely the scholarly term "of one substance" that defends that guileless simplicity of which the Lord speaks when he says: "I thank thee, Father, Lord of heaven and earth, that thou hast hidden these things from the wise and understanding and revealed them to babes" (Mt 11:25; cf. 1 Pet 2:2).[15]

Thesis 6: The so-called Neo-Chalcedonian theology which is summed up in the Third Council of Constantinople (680–681) makes an important contribution to a proper grasp of the inner unity of biblical and dogmatic theology, of theology and religious life. Only from this standpoint does the dogma of Chalcedon (451) yield its full meaning.

It is common enough for the theological textbooks to pay scant attention to the theological development which followed Chalcedon. In many ways one is left with the impression that dogmatic Christology comes to a stop with a certain parallelism of the two natures in Christ.[16]

[15] Cf. J. Ratzinger, *Der Gott Jesu Christi* (Munich 1976), 70–76; on the historical questions, cf. my article "Emanation", in RAC 4:1219–28; A. Grillmeier, *Christ in Christian Traditon*, 2nd ed. (London 1975), 249–73; W. Kasper, *Jesus the Christ* (London 1976); K. Lehmann, "Dogmengeschichtliche Hermeneutik am Beispiel der Christologie des Konzils von Nikäa", in B. Casper et al., *Jesus, Ort der Erfahrung Gottes* (Freiburg 1970), 190–209.

[16] Criticism of this weakness of the Chalcedonian model is a recurring theme in the two works by D. Wiederkehr quoted above (note 2). Since, however, he devotes insufficient attention to the succeeding development in later councils and completely misunderstands Constantinople III, in spite of good observations he comes to no satisfactory solution, especially in relating the Christology of being to that of consciousness, the doctrine of the Son to the biblical witness to the Son's experience. With regard to this fundamental issue, a correct interpretation of Constantinople is crucial.

It was this same impression that led to the divisions in the wake of Chalcedon. In fact, however, the affirmation of the true humanity and the true divinity in Christ can only retain its meaning if the mode of the unity of both is clarified. The Council defined this unity by speaking of the "one Person" in Christ, but it was a formula which remained to be explored in its implications.[17] For the unity of divinity and humanity in Christ which brings "salvation" to man is not a juxtaposition but a mutual indwelling. Only in this way can there be that genuine "becoming like God", without which there is no liberation and no freedom.

It was to this question, after two centuries of dramatic struggles which also, in many ways, bore the mark of imperial politics, that the Third Council of Constantinople (680–681) addressed itself. On the one hand, it teaches that the unity of God and man in Christ involves no amputation or reduction in any way of human nature. In conjoining himself to man, his creature, God does not violate or diminish him; in doing so, he brings him for the first time to his real fullness. On the other hand (and this is no less important), it abolishes all dualism or parallelism of the two natures, such as had always seemed necessary in order to safeguard Jesus' human freedom. In such attempts it had been forgotten that when the human will is taken up into the will of God, freedom is not destroyed; indeed, only then does genuine freedom come into its own. The Council of Constantinople analyzed the question of the two-ness and the one-ness in Christ by reference to the concrete issue of the will of Jesus. It resolutely maintains that, as

[17] On the complicated history of the gradual exploration of the Chalcedonian formula, cf. A. Grillmeier, *Mit ihm und in ihm* (Freiburg 1975), 283–300; 355–70.

man, Jesus has a human will which is not absorbed by the divine will. But this human will follows the divine will and thus becomes one will with it, not in a natural manner but along the path of freedom. The metaphysical two-ness of a human and a divine will is not abrogated, but in the realm of the *person*, in the realm of freedom, the fusion of both takes place, with the result that they become *one* will, not naturally, but personally. This free unity—a form of unity created by love—is higher and more interior than a merely natural unity. It corresponds to the highest unity there is, namely, trinitarian unity. The Council illustrates this unity by citing a dominical word handed down to us in the Gospel of John: "I have come down from heaven, not to do my own will, but the will of him who sent me" (Jn 6:38). Here it is the divine Logos who is speaking, and he speaks of the human will of the man Jesus as his will, the will of the Logos. With this exegesis of John 6:38 the Council indicates the unity of the subject in Christ. There are not two "I"'s in him, but only one. The Logos speaks in the I-form of the human will and mind of Jesus; it has become his I, has become adopted into his I, because the human will is completely one with the will of the Logos. United with the latter, it has become a pure Yes to the Father's will.[18]

[18] The Council text can be found in J. Alberigo et al., *Conciliorum oecumeniorum decreta*, 2nd ed. (Bologna 1973), 124–30. The intellectual (and political) factors which led to the Council and influenced it are concisely and accurately presented by J. Beck in H. Jedin (ed.), *Handbuch der Kirchengeschichte II*, 2 (Freiburg 1975): 39–43. The central distinction which is fundamental to the Council (and which has received scant attention up to now) was worked out by Maximus the Confessor: he distinguishes the θέλημα φυσικόν which belongs to the nature and thus exists separately in Christ's godhead and manhood, from the "gnomic" θέλημα "which is identical with the *liberum arbitrium* and pertains to the person; in Christ it can only be a single

Maximus the Confessor, the great theological inter-
preter of this second phase of the development of the

θέλημα, since he subsists in the divine Person" (Beck 41). Thus "much
that had earlier been regarded as Monophysite . . . could be taken
into spirituality" (Beck 43). Once this basic idea of Constantinople III,
which is central to Neo-Chalcedonian Christology, has been grasped,
it becomes clear that Wiederkehr's attacks on Neo-Chalcedonian
Christology, based on Pannenberg, are futile, resting on a misunderstanding. In *Theol. Berichte* 2:29, Wiederkehr speaks of the "symmetrical path of the two-natures doctrine" under the influence of the
"two-wills" decision and thinks that it resulted from the idea "of an
internal christological dialogue . . . between a divine and a human
nature". Thus he can rightly object that "there is nothing of this in the
Jesus of the synoptics". "As far as the man Jesus is concerned, his
dialogue partner is the Father, not his own self in his divine nature and
person." This assertion, which he opposes to Neo-Chalcedonism, is
in fact precisely the view of Constantinople III, except that the latter
works out its ontological and existential structure very much more
thoroughly than Wiederkehr. Pannenberg (*Jesus, God and Man*, 1968)
formulates it thus: " 'Person' is a relational concept, and, because the
relation of Jesus to the Father in his dedication to him is identical with
the relation to the Father intended by the designation 'the Son', Jesus
in his human dedication to the Father is identical with the eternal
Person of the Son of God" (339). It seems to me, if I read him
correctly, that Pannenberg too fails to see that he is thinking along the
same lines as Constantinople III (and Maximus the Confessor). In fact
he is concentrating rather on the dispute with Leontius of Byzantium.
From the point of view of the history of ideas, Wiederkehr's insistent
opposition to the "internal christological" and "symmetrical" concept of the two-natures model, in favor of a relational trinitarian
Christology, is interesting in that it brusquely rejects what K. Rahner
had proclaimed in 1954, in support of Galtier. At that time, in
opposition to what he saw as the faithful's actual monotheletism, he
put forward a radical "two-wills" position which had apparently lost
sight of the unity of the "gnomic" will in Jesus. This introduced a
split in the person which neither had biblical foundation nor was
philosophically intelligible ("Chalkedon—Ende oder Anfang?" in
A. Grillmeier–H. Bacht, *Das Konzil von Chalkedon III* [Würzburg
1954], 3–49, esp. 13).

christological dogma, illuminates this whole context by reference to Jesus' prayer on the Mount of Olives, which, as we already saw in Thesis 1, expresses Jesus' unique relationship to God. Indeed, it is as if we were actually looking in on the inner life of the Word-made-man. It is revealed to us in the sentence which remains the measure and model of all real prayer: "Not what I will, but what thou wilt" (Mk 14:36).[19] Jesus' human will assimilates itself to the will of the Son. In doing this, he receives the Son's identity, i.e., the complete subordination of the I to the Thou, the self-giving and self-expropriation of the I to the Thou. This is the very essence of him who is pure relation and pure act. Wherever the I gives itself to the Thou, there is freedom because this involves the reception of the "form of God".

But we can also describe this process, and describe it better, from the other side: the Logos so humbles himself that he adopts a man's will as his own and addresses the Father with the I of this human being; he transfers his own I to this man and thus transforms human speech into the eternal Word, into his blessed "Yes, Father". By imparting his own I, his own identity, to this human being, he liberates him, redeems him, makes him God. Now we can take the real meaning of "God has become man" in both hands, as it were: the Son transforms the anguish of a man into his own filial obedience, the speech of the servant into the Word which is the Son.

---

[19] I find it interesting that Constantinople III here uses the same scriptural text quoted by Pope Honorius, correcting (or developing) his view by relating the text to the gnomic will. For further light on the interpretation of the Council, cf. A. Miralles, "Precisiones terminológicas entorno al misterio de Cristo sugeridas por la lectura de los Concilios I y III de Constantinopla", in L. F. Mateo-Seco (ed.), *Cristo, Hijo de Dios y Redentor del Hombre* (Pamplona 1982), 597–606.

Thus we come to grasp the manner of our liberation, our participation in the Son's freedom. As a result of the unity of wills of which we have spoken, the greatest possible change has taken place in man, the only change which meets his desire: he has become divine. We can therefore describe that prayer which enters into the praying of Jesus and becomes the prayer of Jesus in the Body of Christ as freedom's laboratory. Here and nowhere else takes place that radical change in man of which we stand in need, that the world may become a better place. For it is only along this path that conscience attains its fundamental soundness and its unshakable power. And only from such a conscience can there come that ordering of human affairs which corresponds to human dignity and protects it. Every generation has to seek anew this right ordering of the world in response to a conscience that is alert, until the kingdom of God comes, which God alone can establish.

Thesis 7: The historico-critical method and other modern scientific methods are important for an understanding of Holy Scripture and tradition. Their value, however, depends on the hermeneutical (philosophical) context in which they are applied.

In the interpretation of Holy Scripture we are in danger today of divorcing scholarship from tradition, reason from faith. Many people are under the impression that historico-critical exegesis destroys faith. On the other side the view gains ground that critical exegesis is the real teaching office, subordinate to no other authority. The believer is convinced that there cannot be any contradiction between reason and faith if both are exercised properly. Without reason, faith would not be truly human; without faith, reason has neither a path nor a guiding light.

The historico-critical method is essentially a tool, and its usefulness depends on the way in which it is used, i.e., on the hermeneutical and philosophical presuppositions one adopts in applying it.[20] In fact there is no such thing as a pure historical method; it is always carried on in a hermeneutical or philosophical context, even when people are not aware of it or expressly deny it. The difficulties which faith continually experiences today in the face of critical exegesis do not stem from the historical or critical factors as such but from the latent philosophy which is at work. The argument, therefore, must relate to this underlying philosophy; it must not attempt to bring historical thought as such under suspicion. Historically speaking, this method was first applied to the Gospels at the time of the Enlightenment, with the aim of using history to correct dogma, setting up a purely human, historical Jesus against the Christ of faith. Since then the method has undergone much change and has played a part in quite diverse scenarios. Again and again, competent scholars have purged it of these rationalistic intentions, and it has yielded very many important insights, enhancing our understanding of the biblical testi-

[20] The question of method can only be dealt with very generally here. It seemed appropriate, however, to make some basic reference to the way in which method and hermeneutics are interwoven. Cf. *Theol. Quartalschrift*, 159 (1979), fasc. 1, with contributions by Blank, Küng, Kasper, B. Lang, H. J. Vogt and others; L. Scheffczyk, *Die Theologie und die Wissenschaften* (Aschaffenburg 1979); P. Stuhlmacher, "Thesen zur Methodologie gegenwärtiger Exegese", in ZNW 63 (1972): 18–26. An important book offering criticism of modern exegetical positions is R. Blank, *Analyse und Kritik der formgeschichtlichen Arbeiten von M. Dibelius und R. Bultmann* (Basel 1981).

mony and of the saving history which it contains. However, where the Enlightenment line is pursued, new divorces follow with inner inevitability from the original separation of Jesus and Christ. Since the inner unity of the books of the New Testament, and that of the two Testaments, can only be seen in the light of faith's interpretation, where this is lacking, people are forever separating out new components and discovering contradictions in the sources. Then, as a result, the figure of Jesus also is continually splitting into new pictures of Jesus: there is the Jesus of the logia, the Jesus of this or that community, Jesus the philanthropist, Jesus the Jewish rabbi, the apocalyptic Jesus, Jesus the Zealot, Jesus the revolutionary, the political Jesus, etc. In all these cases some preconceived idea determines the principles of interpretation; once these have been adopted, the historical method is applied, with varying degrees of care and subtlety, in order to try to prove, to oneself and to others, that the Jesus of one's own preconceptions is the only possible historical Jesus. In reality this process of dividing-up only reflects the divisions in man's mind and in the world; indeed, the process only serves to intensify them. But Jesus did not come to divide the world but to unite it (cf. Eph 2:11–22). It is the one who "gathers" with Jesus, who works against the process of scattering, ruin and dismemberment, who finds the real Jesus (cf. Lk 11:23).

Here, at any rate, we come face to face with the question of which hermeneutics actually leads to truth and how it can demonstrate its legitimacy. We cannot go into the question in great detail, but I would like to indicate the general line of approach. From a purely scientific point of view, the legitimacy of an interpretation depends on its power to explain things. In other words, the less it needs to interfere with the sources, the more it respects the corpus as given and is able to show it to be intelligible from within, by its own logic, the more apposite such an interpretation is. Conversely, the more it interferes with the sources, the more it feels obliged to excise and throw doubt on things found there, the more alien to the subject it is. To that extent, its explanatory power is also its ability to maintain the inner unity of the corpus in question. It involves the ability to unify, to achieve a synthesis, which is the reverse of superficial harmonization. Indeed, only faith's hermeneutic is sufficient to measure up to these criteria. It has a twofold unifying power:

1. It is the only hermeneutics which is in a position to hold fast the entire testimony of the sources; it is also the only one which is able to comprehend the sources' different nuances and their pluriformity, because it alone has a vision of unity which is wide enough to accommodate the apparent contradictions; nothing needs to be excluded on the grounds of its being a hostile development which cannot be integrated into the whole. Only the doctrine of the two natures joined together in one Person is able to open up a vista in which the apparent contradictions found in the tradition each have enough scope and can be molded together into a totality. Every other view of the figure of Jesus is partial; it has to absolutize a portion of the sources, or even manufacture sources behind the sources, if it is to survive. This always involves throwing doubt on some part of the historical corpus.

2. Faith's hermeneutics is also the only medium which, in the breadth of its vision, transcends the differences of cultures, times and peoples. It does not alienate any civilization, any people, from its own values. In the

higher unity of the incarnate Word they can all find their place, cultivate what is distinctively theirs and, through the refining influence of this faith, discover the true depth it possesses. Such a hermeneutics can also surmount all the divisions which tear the world to pieces and can initiate a spiritual fellowship in which everything belongs to everyone and there is a mutual relationship of giving and receiving, because of him who has given us himself and, in and with himself, the whole fullness of God.

If we had space to follow these thoughts, we could show faith's fruitfulness, which does not violate the historical record but reveals its truth and is open to every genuine truth. The unity of the person of Jesus, embracing man and God, prefigures that synthesis of man and world to which theology is meant to minister. It is my belief that the beauty and necessity of the theologian's task could be made visible at this point. He would be bringing to light the foundations for a possible unity in a world marked by divisions. He must seek to answer the question of how this unity can be recognized and brought about today. In this way he could be contributing to prepare for that unity which is the locus of both freedom and salvation. But he can only do this provided he himself enters that "laboratory" of unity and freedom of which we have spoken, i.e., where his own will is refashioned, where he allows himself to be expropriated and inserted into the divine will, where he advances toward that God-likeness through which the kingdom of God can come. Thus we have arrived back at our starting point: Christology is born of prayer or not at all.

The Mystery of Easter

Substance and Foundation of Devotion to the Sacred Heart

I. The Crisis in Devotion to the Sacred Heart In the Age of Liturgical Reform

Although the encyclical *Haurietis aquas* was written at a time when devotion to the Sacred Heart was still alive in the forms of the nineteenth century, a crisis in this kind of devotion was already clearly detectable. More and more, the spirituality of the liturgical movement was dominating the Church's spiritual climate in Central Europe; this spirituality, drawing its nourishment from the classical shape of the Roman liturgy, deliberately turned its back on the emotionalistic piety of the nineteenth century and its symbolism. It saw its model in the strict form of the Roman *orationes*, in which feeling is restrained and there is an extreme sobriety of expression, free of all subjectivity. Along with this went a theological cast of mind which wanted to steer entirely by Scripture and the Fathers, fashioning itself equally strictly according to the objective structural laws of the Christian edifice. The more emotional emphases of modern times were to be subordinated once more within this objective form.

A paper given to the Sacred Heart Congress in Toulouse, July 24–28, 1981, commemorating the twenty-fifth anniversary of the encyclical *Haurietis aquas*.

This meant, first and foremost, that Marian piety as well as those modern forms of prayer of a christological stamp, the Stations of the Cross and devotion to the Sacred Heart, had to retire into the background or else look for new modes of expression.

Since the rise of the biblical and liturgical movement, attempts had also been taken in hand to reveal and deepen the biblical and patristic basis both of devotion to the Sacred Heart and of Marian piety in order to preserve the inheritance of more recent ages of the Church and involve it in the return to Christian origins. Hugo Rahner deserves special mention in the German-speaking area, for he uncovered the connection between Mary and the Church in the theology of the Fathers and was thus one of the first to prepare a way for the Mariology of the Second Vatican Council.[1] He endeavored to provide a new basis for devotion to the Sacred Heart by connecting it with the way the Fathers had interpreted John 7:37–39 and John 19:34.[2] Both passages are concerned with the opened side of Jesus, with the blood and water which flow from it. Both passages are an expression of the Paschal Mystery: from the Lord's pierced Heart proceeds the life-giving stream of the sacraments; the grain of wheat, dying, becomes the new ear, carrying the fruit of the Church forward through the ages. Both texts also express the connection between Christology and pneumatology: the water of life which springs from the Lord's side is the Holy Spirit, the spring of life which makes the desert blossom. This also brings out the connection between Christology, pneumatology and

---

[1] Cf. esp. *Maria und die Kirche* (Innsbruck 1951); *Mater Ecclesia. Lobpreis der Kirche aus dem ersten Jahrtausend* (Einsiedeln 1944).

[2] The relevant articles are collected in H. Rahner, *Symbole der Kirche. Die Ekklesiologie der Väter* (Salzburg 1964), 177–235.

ecclesiology: Christ communicates himself to us in the Holy Spirit; and it is the Holy Spirit who makes the clay into a living Body, i.e., fuses isolated men into the one organism of the love of Jesus Christ. It is also the Holy Spirit who imparts new meaning to Adam's becoming "one flesh" with Eve, applying it to the Second Adam: "He who is united to the Lord becomes one spirit with him" (1 Cor 6:17). The liturgical movement had discovered the center of Christian spirituality in the Paschal Mystery. In his researches, Hugo Rahner had tried to show that devotion to the Sacred Heart, too, is nothing but devotion to the mystery of Easter and thus concentrates on the core of Christian faith.

The encyclical *Haurietis aquas* begins with that prophetic word of Isaiah 12:3, of which the Lord proclaims himself to be the fulfillment in his Easter mystery in John 7:37–39. Thus its very opening words link up with the efforts of men like Hugo Rahner: it too was concerned to overcome the dangerous dualism between liturgical spirituality and nineteenth-century devotion, to let each of them stimulate the other to bring forth fruit, to bring them into a fruitful relationship without simply dissolving the one in the other. The encyclical was evidently aware that the reflections of Hugo Rahner alone would not suffice to provide a new basis for devotion to the Sacred Heart and to ensure its continued vitality. Doubtless Hugo Rahner had made it abundantly clear that devotion to the Sacred Heart is in touch with a central biblical reality—that it is an Easter spirituality. He had shown that tremendous picture of the opened side of Jesus, from which blood and water flow, and laid it before the spiritual eyes of Christianity's Sacred Heart devotion, as the new devotional image, as it were, the biblical icon. Thus he had invited people, in meditating on this picture, to fulfill the word of the prophet Zechariah (12:10) which John himself quotes in this context: "They shall look on him whom they have pierced" (cf. Jn 19:37; Rev 1:7; also Jn 3:14). Yet two objections remain which Rahner did not deal with:

1. The two passages in John 7 and John 19, on which he focused as the biblical basis of devotion to the Sacred Heart, do not mention the word "heart". The person who accepts devotion to the Sacred Heart as a reality in the Church can discover in these texts its inner ground and its most profound substance, since in fact they interpret the mystery of the heart. Of themselves, however, they cannot explain why it is the Lord's *Heart* that is the center of the Easter image.

2. But a more radical question can be asked. If devotion to the Sacred Heart is a mode of Paschal spirituality, what is there that is specific to it? Surely it is superfluous to behold the Easter mystery in an emotional way, in a devotional image, when it is possible actually to participate in it where it is really present *in mysterio*, in the sacraments, i.e., in the Church's liturgy? Surely this devotional empathizing, this emotional way of making the Easter mystery real, is a secondary form of Christian spirituality, a secondary form of mysticism, compared with the primary mysticism of the "mystery", i.e., the liturgy? Did it not arise simply because people no longer had a sense of this primary mysticism, no longer understood it in the fossilization of the old liturgy? Is it not doomed once this liturgy comes to life again?

II. The Encyclical *Haurietis aquas* Indicates The Elements of a New Rationale for Devotion to the Sacred Heart

Questions such as these, in the wake of the Council, led to the idea that everything expressed prior to the liturgical reform was now invalidated. And in fact they brought about the disappearance, to a large extent, of devotion to the Sacred Heart. This is of course a misunderstanding of Vatican II: the encyclical *Haurietis aquas* replied to these very questions, and in terms which were presupposed, not superseded, in the Council's liturgical reform. So it is not merely the fact that twenty-five years have passed since this encyclical appeared that causes us to give it fresh thought; the state of the Church's spirituality itself calls for it. My reflections simply trace the encyclical's basic answers to these questions, clarifying and drawing out somewhat, in the light of subsequent theological work, the lines there developed.

1. The devotion's foundation in a theology of the Incarnation

The encyclical develops an anthropology and a theology of bodily existence, which it regards as the philosophical and psychological basis of the cult of the Heart of Jesus. The body is not something external to the spirit, it is the latter's self-expression, its "image". The constituents of biological life are also constitutive of the human person. The person exercises personhood in the body, and the body is thus the mode of expression; the invisible presence of the spirit can be discerned in it. Since the body is the visible form of the person, and the person is the image of God, it follows that the body, in its whole context of relationships, is the place where the divine is portrayed, uttered and rendered accessible to our gaze. Thus, from the very beginning, the Bible represents the mystery of God in the metaphors of the body and its world. In doing so, it is not making graven images for God, extrinsically, but using bodily things as illustrations, speaking of God in parables, because all these things *are* genuinely images. Thus Scripture, in speaking in parables, far from distancing itself from the bodily world, actually addresses itself to it as what is most its own, as the core of what it itself is. By interpreting the bodily world as a store of images for God's history with man, Scripture illuminates its true nature and makes God visible at the place where he really expresses himself. This is the context, too, in which the Bible understands the Incarnation. The taking up of the human world, of the human person expressed in the body, into the biblical word, its transformation into parable and imagery of the divine by means of the biblical proclamation, is a kind of anticipation of the Incarnation. In the Incarnation of the Logos we have the fulfillment of something that has been underway ever since the very beginning in biblical history. It is as if the Word has continually been drawing flesh toward itself, making it its *own* flesh, the sphere of its own self. On the one hand the Incarnation can only take place because the flesh has always been the Spirit's outward expression and hence a possible dwelling for the Word; on the other hand it is only the Son's Incarnation that imparts to man and the visible world their ultimate and innermost meaning.[3]

[3] Encyclical *Haurietas aquas*, AAS 38 (1956):316f.; cf. 327; 336; 334 350. What was new in this encyclical, as compared with previous rationales, is very well presented in F. Hausmann, "*Haurietas aquas*.

With this philosophy and theology of corporality the encyclical complements the Easter aspect which, in Hugo Rahner for instance, had tended to dominate. The Incarnation, certainly, does not exist for its own sake; of its very nature it is ordered to transcendence and hence to the dynamism of the Easter mystery. Its whole basis is the fact that, in his paradoxical love, God transcends himself and enters the realm of flesh, the realm of the passion of the human being. Conversely, however, this self-transcendence on the part of God only serves to bring to light that inner transcendence of the entire creation which the Creator himself has appointed: body is the self-transcending movement toward spirit, and, through the spirit, to God. Beholding the invisible in the visible is an Easter phenomenon. The encyclical sees it summed up in John 20:26–29: doubting Thomas, who needs to be able to see and touch before he can believe, puts his hand into the Lord's opened side; in touching, he recognizes what is beyond touch and yet actually does touch it; he beholds the invisible and yet really sees it: "My Lord and my God" (20:28). The encyclical illustrates this with the beautiful passage from Bonaventure's *Mystical Vine*, which is a cardinal element of devotion to the Sacred Heart: "The wound of the body also reveals the spiritual wound. . . . Let us look through the visible wound to the invisible wound of love!"[4]

Ultimately, then, everything here has an Easter orienta-

_____

Marginalien zum dogmatischen Verständnis der Herz-Jesu-Verehrung in der Herz-Jesu-Enzyklika Papst Pius' XII", in J. Auer–F. Mussner– G. Schwaiger *Gottesherrschaft–Weltherrschaft* (Festschrift R. Graber) (Regensburg 1980), 279–94.

[4] Bonaventure, *Vitis mystica* c 3, 4 (ed. Quaracchi VIII 163 b); cf. *Haurietas aquas*, 337.

tion. But we can discern the basis of the Easter mystery, the ontological and psychological situation it presupposes; namely, the connection of body and spirit, of Logos, Spirit and body, making the incarnate Logos into a "ladder" which we can climb as we behold, touch and experience. All of us are Thomas, unbelieving; but, like him, all of us can touch the exposed Heart of Jesus and thus touch and behold the Logos himself. So, with our hands and eyes fixed upon this Heart, we can attain to the confession of faith: "My Lord and my God!"

2. The importance of the senses and the emotions in spirituality

What we have just said has already indicated the lines of the conclusion drawn by the encyclical on the basis of its theology of corporality and of the Incarnation: man needs to see, he needs this kind of silent beholding which becomes a touching, if he is to become aware of the mysteries of God. He must set his foot on the "ladder" of the body in order to climb it and so find the path along which faith invites him. From the point of view of our contemporary problems, we could put it like this: the so-called objective spirituality, which is based on participation in the celebration of the liturgy, is not enough. The extraordinary spiritual depth which resulted from medieval mysticism and the ecclesially based piety of modern times cannot be abandoned as obsolete (let alone deviant) in the name of a rediscovery of the Bible and the Fathers. The liturgy itself can only be celebrated properly if it is prepared for, and accompanied by, that meditative "abiding" in which the heart begins to see and to understand, drawing the senses too into its beholding. For "you only see properly with your heart", as Saint-Exupéry's Little Prince says. (And the Little Prince can be taken as a symbol for that childlikeness which we must regain if we are to find our way back out of the clever foolishness of the adult world and into man's true nature, which is beyond mere reason.)

The theology of corporality which the encyclical puts forward is also, therefore, an apologia for the heart, the senses and the emotions—precisely in the realm of spirituality. The encyclical bases itself in part on Ephesians 3:18f.: "that you . . . may have power to comprehend with all the saints what is the breadth and length and height and depth, and to know the love of Christ which surpasses knowledge. . . ." As long ago as the Fathers, in particular in the pseudo-Dionysian tradition, this passage had led theologians to stress that reason had its limits. This is the origin, in the latter tradition, of the *ignote cognoscere*, knowing in unknowing, which leads to the concept of *docta ignorantia*; thus the mysticism of darkness comes about where love alone is able to see.[5] Many texts could be quoted here, for instance, Gregory the Great's *"Amor ipse notitia est"*; Hugh of St. Victor's *"Intrat dilectio et appropinquat, ubi scientia foris est"*; or Richard of St. Victor's beautiful formulation: *"Amor oculus est et amare videre est"* ("love is the eye, and to love is to see").[6] The encyclical concentrates, however, on verse 18, the "breadth and length and height and depth" and interprets it like this:

"We must realize that God's love is not only spiritual." The Old Testament, particularly in the Psalms and the

[5] On this, cf. the important analyses in E. von Ivánka, *Plato christianus* (Einsiedeln 1964), 309–85.

[6] PL 196:1203. Cf. Ivánka, 309, 335.

Song of Songs, bears witness to an entirely spiritual love, "whereas the love which addresses us in the Gospel, the Acts and the Apocalypse . . . expresses not merely divine love but also the tangible form of human love . . . for God's Word did not assume an imaginary and inconsequential body".[7]

Here, therefore, we are explicitly invited to enter into a spirituality involving the senses, corresponding to the bodily nature of the divine-human love of Jesus Christ. In the terms of the encyclical, however, spirituality of the senses is essentially a spirituality of the heart, since the heart is the hub of all the senses, the place where sense and spirit meet, interpenetrate and unite. Spirituality of the senses is spirituality in the sense of Cardinal Newman's motto: *Cor ad cor loquitur* (heart speaks to heart), which sums up, in perhaps the most beautiful way, what spirituality of the heart is, a spirituality focused on the Heart of Jesus.

The encyclical adds another important set of motifs to these reflections on the tradition of devotion to the Sacred Heart. For the heart is an expression for the human πάθη (passions)—i.e., not only man's passions but also the "passion" of being human. Over against the Stoic ideal of *apatheia*, over against the Aristotelian God, who is Thought thinking itself, the heart is the epitome of the passions, without which there could have been no Passion on the part of the Son. The encyclical cites Justin, Basil, Chrysostom, Ambrose, Jerome, Augustine, John Damascene, exhibiting different variations of the same theme, which it sees as common ground in patristic Christology: . . . *passionum nostrarum particeps factus est*

[7] *Haurietis aquas* II, 322f.

(he has come to share in our "passions").[8] For the Fathers, who were brought up with the moral ideal of the Stoa, the ideal of the wise man's impassivity, where insight and the will govern and master the irrational emotions, this was one of the places where it proved most difficult to achieve a synthesis of Greek inheritance and biblical faith. The God of the Old Testament, with his wrath, compassion and love, often seemed nearer to the gods of the obsolete religions than to the lofty concept of God of the ancient philosophy, a concept which had facilitated the breakthrough of monotheism in the Mediterranean world. From the vantage point of Cicero's Hortensius, Augustine could not find the way back to the Bible; thus there was a very strong temptation to adopt the Gnosticism which separated the God of the Old Testament from the God of the New Covenant. On the other hand, however, it was plain enough that the figure of Jesus, who experiences anguish and anger, joy, hope and despair, is in the Old Testament tradition of God; in him who is the incarnate Logos, the anthropomorphisms of the Old Testament are radicalized and attain their ultimate depth of meaning. The Docetic attempt to make Jesus' sufferings a mere surface illusion was an option congenial to Stoic thought. But it must be clear to every unprejudiced reader of the Bible that such an option would attack the very heart of the biblical testimony to Christ, i.e., the mystery of Easter. It was impossible to excise Christ's sufferings, but there can be no Passion without passions: suffering presupposes the ability to suffer, it presupposes the faculty of the emotions. In the period of the Fathers it was doubtless

[8] *Haurietis aquas*, ibid., 325f. The text quoted is Justin, *Apol II*, 13 (PG 6:465).

Origen who grasped most profoundly the idea of the suffering God and made bold to say that it could not be restricted to the suffering humanity of Jesus but also affected the Christian picture of God. The Father suffers in allowing the Son to suffer, and the Spirit shares in this suffering, for Paul says that he groans within us, yearning in us and on our behalf for full redemption (Rom 8:26f.).[9] And it was Origen also who gave the normative definition of the way in which the theme of the suffering God is to be interpreted: When you hear someone speak of God's passions, always apply what is said to love.[10] So God is a sufferer because he is a lover; the entire theme of the suffering God flows from that of the loving God and always points back to it. The actual advance registered by the Christian idea of God over that of the ancient world lies in its recognition that God is love.[11]

[9] Cf. Origen, *Ezech.* h. 6, 6 (Baehr. VIII 384f.): ". . . The Father himself is not without feeling (*impassibilis*). When we cry to him, he has mercy and shares in the experience of suffering; because of love he tastes something which, from the point of view of his sublimity, he cannot experience." Gregory Nazianzen writes similarly in his poem on human nature, V. 121f. (PG 37:765). For an interpretation of these texts, cf. H. U. von Balthasar, *Das Ganze im Fragment* (Einsiedeln 1963), 300f. On the "passion" of the Spirit, cf. the profound interpretation of Romans 8:26 in H. Schlier, *Der Römerbrief* (Freiburg 1977), 268ff.

[10] Cf. H. de Lubac, *Histoire et esprit: l'intelligence de l'Écriture d'après Origène* (1950). De Lubac situates Origen in the history of biblical interpretation. He finds a parallel and a development of the ideas of the Alexandrian scholar in Bernard of Clairvaux's beautiful dictum: *impassibilis est Deus, sed non incompassibilis* (*In Cant. cant.* 26, n. 5 PL 183:906); he regards Pascal's "Everything that does not tend toward charity is a figure" (*Pensées* 583) as central even to Origen's hermeneutics.

[11] This must be made absolutely clear, lest the way be opened for a new Patripassianism, as J. Moltmann seems to be proposing in *The Crucified God* (London 1974). On this particular issue, cf. H. U. von Balthasar, "Zu einer christlichen Theologie der Hoffnung",

The topic of the suffering God has become almost fashionable today, not without reason, as a result of the abandonment of a theology which was one-sidedly rationalist and as a result of the rejection of a portrait of Jesus and a concept of God which had been emasculated, where the love of God had degenerated into the cheap platitude of a God who was merely kind, and hence "harmless".[12] Against such a backdrop Christianity is diminished to the level of philanthropic world improvement, and Eucharist becomes a brotherly meal. The theme of the suffering God can only stay sound if it is anchored in love for God and in prayerful attention to his love. The encyclical *Haurietis aquas* sees the passions of Jesus, which are summed up and set forth in the Heart, as the basis, as the reason why, the human heart, i.e., the capacity for feeling, the emotional side of love, must be

---

in *MThZ* 32 (1981): 81–102. An important book arising from the recent debate on the pain of God is J. Galot, *Dieu souffre-t-il?* (Paris 1976). H. U. von Balthasar sums up the present position in *Theodramatik IV (Das Endspiel)* (Einsiedeln 1983), 191–222. Like Galot, Balthasar refers in this connection to a remarkable treatise by J. Maritain, entitled "Quelques réflexions sur le savoir théologique", in *Rev Thom* 77 (1969): 5–27. Von Balthasar (239) cites the following sentence from it: "God 'suffers' with us, and in doing so he suffers more than we do; as long as there is suffering in the world, he shares this suffering, he experiences 'com-passion'." This once again takes up St. Bernard's line of thought: *impassibilis–sed non incompassibilis* (see note 10 above), which alone is inadequate, in my view, to Scripture and tradition. The papal encyclical *Dives in misericordia* (1980) takes up the very same point (n.b. its highly significant note 52) and seizes upon the central element uniting theo-logy, Christology and anthropology. An important article on the philosophical issues here is M. Gervais, "Incarnation et immuabilité divine", in *Rev des Sciences Rel* 50 (1976): 215–43.

[12] Cf. H. Kuhn, "Woran man sich halten kann", in *MThZ* 30 (1979): 49–52.

drawn into man's relationship with God. Incarnational spirituality must be a spirituality of the passions, a spirituality of "heart to heart"; in that way, precisely, it is an Easter spirituality, for the mystery of Easter, the mystery of suffering, is of its very nature a mystery of the heart.

Developments since the Council have confirmed this view on the part of the encyclical. Theology today is certainly no longer confronted with a Stoic ethos of *apatheia*, but it is faced with a technological rationalism which pushes man's emotional side to the irrational periphery and allots a merely instrumental role to the body. Accordingly, the emotions are placed under a kind of taboo in spirituality, only to be followed by a wave of emotionalism which is, however, largely chaotic and incapable of commitment. We could say that the taboo on pathos renders it pathological, whereas the real issue is how to integrate it into the totality of human existence, the totality of our life as we stand before God. Similarly, the neglect of a meditative, contemplative spirituality in favor of an exclusive, community-based activism has produced a wave of meditation which largely dissociates itself from the specifically Christian content, or even finds the latter a hindrance. These developments show how much has collapsed in the life of the Church at the very moment when people thought they could cast aside the entire spirituality of the second Christian millennium as being of no account, thinking they should be satisfied with what was imagined to be the pure spirituality of the Bible and of the early centuries.

3. The anthropology and theology of the heart in the Bible and the Fathers

All this shows that Christian spirituality involves the senses, which are structured by and united in the heart, and the emotions, which are focused on the heart. We have shown that this kind of heart-centered spirituality corresponds to the picture of the Christian God who has a heart. We have shown that all this is ultimately the expression and elucidation of the Paschal Mystery which sums up God's love story with man. However, we must go on to ask whether this emphasis on the word "heart" accords, not only with the issue itself, but also with the language of the inherited tradition. For, if the concept "heart" is as fundamental as we have shown it to be, the word itself must have a firm foothold, at least, in the Bible and tradition. In reply I would like to offer two observations:

a. As far as I have been able to ascertain, it was above all the language of the Song of Songs which was the determining factor in the development of medieval mysticism, e.g., phrases such as "You have ravished my heart" (4:9) or the verse quoted by the encyclical, "Set me as a seal upon your heart . . . for love is as strong as death" (8:16). The Fathers, like the great theologians and men of prayer of the Middle Ages, saw the impassioned language of this love song as expressing the theme of God's love for the Church and the soul and also that of man's response. Words such as these were thus fitted to integrate all the passion of human love into man's relationship with God. To the extent that, in modern times, under the dominant influence of a straitened historical mode of thought, people lost the ability to enter into this movement of transcendence whereby the words lead out to mystery, the source itself dried up. To that extent, the possibility of a renewal of the Church and spirituality is also dependent on a recovery of that understanding of the Bible as a whole, in its historical movement, which, because of one or two eccentric manifestations, has wrongly been made taboo (and dismissed as "allegory").[13]

However, rather than pursuing this—which, from a historical point of view, is decisive—I want to mention a passage from the Old Testament where the "heart" theme is quite plain and where the Old Testament's self-transcendence into the New is so obvious as to be unavoidable. I refer to the eleventh chapter of the Book of Hosea, which Heinrich Gross recently put beside 1 Corinthians 13, describing it as "the Canticle of the love of God".[14] The first verses of this chapter portray the immense proportions of the love which God has bestowed on Israel from the very morning of its history: "When Israel was a child, I loved him, and out of Egypt I called my son." But there is no response from the people to this unwearying love of God which is always running after Israel: "The more I called them, the more they went from me . . ." (v. 2). According to the Deuteronomic principle of justice, action like this on man's part must result in a corresponding answer: Israel continually turns away from its vocation; it is always turning around and going back in spite of the Pasch which is intent on saving it. So the sentence is uttered: "They shall return to the

[13] H. de Lubac has presented a thorough discussion of these issues in his book on Origen (see previous note 10). Cf. also H. de Lubac, *Der geistige Sinn der Schrift* (Einsiedeln 1956), reprinted in *Geist aus der Geschichte* (Einsiedeln 1968).

[14] H. Gross, "Das Hohelied der Liebe Gottes", in H. Rossman–J. Ratzinger (ed.), *Mysterium der Gnade (Festschrift J. Auer)* (Regensburg 1975), 83–91.

land of Egypt"—which means, under the prevailing conditions, "Assyria shall be their king" (v. 5); once again Israel will be a banished people, under foreign subjugation. "The sword shall rage against their cities, consume the bars of their gates and devour them in their fortresses" (v. 6). Suddenly, however, a change comes over God's words: Israel may abandon its salvation and deny its election, but can God go back on it? "How can I give you up, O Ephraim! How can I hand you over, O Israel! . . . My heart recoils within me, my compassion grows warm and tender. I will not execute my fierce anger . . . for I am God and not man, the Holy One in your midst, and I will not come to destroy" (v. 8f.).

H. Gross has pointed out that the Old Testament speaks of God's Heart twenty-six times.[15] It is regarded as the organ of his will, against which man is measured. It is because of the pain felt by God's Heart on account of the sins of mankind that he decides to send the Flood. Again, it is the insight into man's weakness on the part of God's Heart that restrains him from ever repeating that kind of judgment. Hosea 11 takes up this line of thought and brings it to a completely new level. God ought to revoke Israel's election and abandon it to its enemies, but "My heart recoils within me, my compassion grows warm and tender". God's Heart turns around—here the Bible uses the same word as in the depiction of God's judgment on the sinful cities of Sodom and Gomorrha (Gen 19:25); the word expresses a total collapse: not one stone remains upon another. The same word is applied to the havoc wrought by love in God's Heart in favor of his people. "The upheaval occasioned in God's Heart by the divine love has the effect of quashing his judicial

---

[15] H. Gross (see previous note), 88; cf. H. W. Wolff, *Anthropologie des Alten Testaments* (Munich 1973), 90–95.

sentence against Israel; God's merciful love conquers his untouchable righteousness (which, in spite of everything, remains untouchable)."[16]

But how can we say that God's righteousness remains untouchable if love has caused such an about-face? Not until the New Testament comes is this made plain. Here we see the upheaval in the Heart of God as God's own, genuine Passion. It consists in God himself, in the person of his Son, suffering Israel's rejection. For in Hosea, God speaks of Israel as "my son", a formula which Matthew will apply to Christ: "Out of Egypt have I called my son" (11:1; Mt 2:15). God takes the destiny of love destroyed upon himself; he takes the place of the sinner and offers the Son's place to men once more, not only to Israel, but to all nations. According to Hosea 11, the Passion of Jesus is the drama of the divine Heart: "My heart recoils within me, my compassion grows warm and tender". The pierced Heart of the crucified Son is the literal fulfillment of the prophecy of the Heart of God, which overthrows its righteousness by mercy and by that very action remains righteous. We can only discern the full magnitude of the biblical message of the Heart of God, the Heart of the divine Redeemer, in this continuity and harmony of Old and New Testament. We see the beginnings of devotion to the Sacred Heart in Bernard of Clairvaux and his circle because at that time the two Testaments were read as a unity; in the Song of Songs of the Old Covenant, people recognized the Canticle of Christ's love for his Church. Today too, we can only appreciate the rationale of the devotion if we receive it once more within the totality of the biblical testimony and so come to comprehend, as Paul urges us, "the breadth and length and height and depth" (Eph 3:18).

[16] H. Gross (see note 14), 89.

b. How do things stand with the Fathers? According to A. Hamon, the first century is silent on the subject of the "Heart of Jesus". Apparently, the word occurs for the first time in Anselm of Canterbury, yet without having acquired its specific meaning.[17] It was Hugo Rahner who, in his analysis of the patristic interpretation of John 7:37–39 and John 19:34, brought the Fathers into the history of devotion to the Sacred Heart. As we have already mentioned, there remains the problem that the Fathers do not use the word "heart" in this context. Now, while it is true that the phrase "Heart of Jesus" apparently does not occur in the Fathers, they do provide, beyond what is indicated by H. Rahner, an important basis for devotion to the Sacred Heart as a result of what can be called their "theology and philosophy of the heart". For the latter is so significant for their whole thought that E. Maxsein, for instance, could publish a study of Augustine's *philosophia cordis*.[18] Anyone who has read his Confessions knows the great part played in it by the word *"cor"* as the center of a dialogical anthropology. It is quite clear that at this point the stream of biblical terminology, and, with it, the stream of biblical theology and anthropology, has entered into his thought and combined with an entirely different, Platonic conception of man, a conception unacquainted with the notion of "heart" in that sense.

We are left with the question of how far a genuine synthesis has been achieved here. Much writing on this subject evinces the suspicion that in the Fathers the biblical world of images and the Platonic world of ideas never actually interpenetrated; Augustine, for instance, one reads, remained largely a Platonist as far as concepts

[17] A. Hamon, "Coeur (Sacré)", in *Dict. de Spiritualité* 2:1023–46.
[18] A. Maxsein, *Philosophia cordis. Das Wesen der Persönlichkeit bei Augustinus* (Salzburg 1966).

were concerned. But people were deeply aware of the problem of the two anthropologies, as we can see from Jerome, who says on one occasion that according to Plato and the Platonists it is the intellect which is the center of man, whereas according to Christ it is the heart.[19] If we examine the matter more closely, it becomes apparent that what we have here is not simply Platonism versus the Bible: the opposition between Platonic and Stoic anthropology is also involved. The tension between these two gave the Fathers the opportunity of drawing on the Bible to create a new anthropological synthesis.[20] In Platonic anthropology it is possible to distinguish individual potencies of the soul, which are related to one another in a hierarchical order: intellect, will, sensibility. Stoic thought, which conceives of man as the microcosm exactly corresponding to the macrocosm, rejects this view; the entire cosmos was fashioned by the primal fire, which is itself formless but adopts the form of that which it creates out of itself. In the same way the human body is fashioned and given life by a spark of this divine, primal fire which permeates it. This single, invigorating energy (πνεῦμα πυρῶδες) transforms itself in accord with the various life functions which serve to preserve and benefit the living being and becomes now hearing, now sight, now thought, now imagination. It is always the same and yet operates in different modes, which implies that there is a kind of ladder of inwardness. The primal fire which sustains the

[19] . . . quaeritur, ubi sit animae principale: Plato in cerebro, Christus monstrat ess in corde. *Epist. 64*, I CSEL 54:587; H. Rahner, in *Symbole der Kirche* (1964), also points out (148) the related passages in Gregory of Nyssa, *De hominis opificio*, c. 12 (PG 44:156 CD) and Lactantius, *De opificio Dei* (CSEL 27:51ff.).

[20] On the following remarks, cf. Ivánka (see note 5), 315–51.

cosmos is called logos; thus its spark in us is called "the logos in us".[21] It is not hard to see the possibilities yielded by these ideas for an understanding of the mystery of Christ. The Stoics had equated this center of the cosmos with the sun, which thus bears the name "heart of the cosmos". Correspondingly the spark of the primal fire in man has its seat in the heart, the organ from which life-giving warmth flows out into the whole organism. The heart is the body's sun, it is the logos in us. Conversely the logos is the heart of the world. Thus Stoic thought has a quite distinctive theology and anthropology of the heart as compared with the intellectualism of the Platonists.[22]

We must describe the view of the Stoics, taken by themselves, as a remarkable amalgam of banal naturalism and profound philosophical intuition. However, they offered the Fathers, engaged in relating the Platonic inheritance to biblical faith, a magnificent opportunity to achieve a new synthesis. And again it was Origen who seized this opportunity most energetically. The signal for him to take up these ideas was the Baptist's word which has come down to us in John 1:26: "Among you stands one whom you do not know." Origen goes on: It is the Logos which is at the center of us all—without our knowing—for the center of man is the heart, and in the heart there is the ἡγεμονικόν—the guiding energy of the whole, which is the Logos.[23] It is the Logos which enables us to be logic-al, to correspond to the Logos; he

[21] Ivánka, 317–21, especially the passages referred to on 321.

[22] Ivánka (364–85) examines in detail the relationship between Platonic, Stoic, Origenist and Augustinian elements in this strand of tradition.

[23] Origen, *in Joa* GCS IV 94, 18; cf. the fragment GCS IV 497f.; Ivánka, 325.

is the image of God after which we were created.[24] Here the word "heart" has expanded beyond the reason and denotes "a deeper level of spiritual/intellectual existence, where direct contact takes place with the divine".[25] It is here, in the heart, that the birth of the divine Logos in man takes place, that man is united with the personal, incarnate Word of God.[26]

E. von Ivánka has given a gripping account of the development, from these lines of thought in Origen, of that stream of spirituality and thought which leads to the start of devotion to the Heart of Jesus in William of St. Thierry and among the German nuns of the Middle Ages and, in more general terms, to that mysticism which is aware that the heart takes precedence over reason, love over knowledge. From there the line continues in a great arch until it reaches Pascal's principle: "*Dieu sensible au coeur, non à la raison.*" "*Le coeur a ses raisons, que la raison ne connaît pas.*"[27] And of course, Newman's motto, "*cor ad cor loquitur*", to which we have already referred, stands in the same continuity.

To that extent, therefore, the view that the heart is the locus of the saving encounter with the Logos has a very firm basis in the new synthesis achieved by patristic thought, as we see, for example, in Augustine's exhortation in connection with the Psalms: *Redeamus ad cor, ut inveniamus Eum* (let us return to the heart, that we may find Him). It would be a very agreeable task to show how, on this basis, the anthropological foundations of

[24] Origen, GCS IV 494, 22ff. On the view which we begin to detect here, of the divine birth from the heart of the Church and the faithful, cf. H. Rahner, *Symbole der Kirche* (see note 2), 13–87.

[25] Ivánka, 326.

[26] Ivánka, 325f.

[27] Ivánka 350.

devotion to the Sacred Heart grow and deepen. Such a task, however, would take us far beyond the limits we have set ourselves here.

One final observation in conclusion: Stoic thought regards the heart as the sun of the microcosm, the life force and preserving energy of the human organism and of man as such. It defines the function of this ἡγεμονικόν, this guiding power, as συντήρησις, as that of holding things together. Cicero puts the meaning of this "holding together" like this: Omne animal . . . id agit, ut se conservet. Seneca expresses it similarly: . . . omnia . . . feruntur in conservationem suam (everything aims at self-preservation).[28] The task of the heart is self-preservation, holding together what is its own. The pierced Heart of Jesus has also truly "overturned" (cf. Hos 11:8) this definition. This Heart is not concerned with self-preservation but with self-surrender. It saves the world by opening itself. The collapse of the opened Heart is the content of the Easter mystery. The Heart saves, indeed, but it saves by giving itself away. Thus, in the Heart of Jesus, the center of Christianity is set before us. It expresses everything, all that is genuinely new and revolutionary in the New Covenant. This Heart calls to our heart. It invites us to step forth out of the futile attempt of self-preservation and, by joining in the task of love, by handing ourselves over to him and with him, to discover the fullness of love which alone is eternity and which alone sustains the world.

[28] References in Ivánka, 320, where he adduces further related texts.

Communion, Community and Mission

On the Connection between Eucharist, (Parish) Community and Mission in the Church

When I was invited to speak on the connection between Eucharist, ecclesial community and the mission of the "parish", the second chapter of Acts (v. 42) immediately sprang to mind. There Luke says that the primitive community "devoted themselves to the Apostles' teaching and fellowship, to the breaking of bread and the prayers". This sentence, it seems to me, offers a real clue to a proper understanding of our question.

First, however, we need to look at the context of Acts and grasp its fundamental purpose. For in this book Luke is writing something like the very first theology of the

This paper was first given during a continuing education course for priests, held in Collevalenza, with the aim of shedding some light on the relationship between Eucharist and "Communità". I started by asking what this word meant: what is "communità"? Is it "community"?—or "fellowship"?—or "communion"?—or all of these at once? Thus it seemed to me that the problem of our sacramental and ecclesiological language arose from the nature of the reality with which it deals. The categories of our language do not correspond to the ways of speaking and thinking which we find in the Bible and the great tradition. A main aim of this paper, therefore, was to demonstrate this and suggest how our speaking and thinking need to be corrected. This being the case, however, how *can* we express the subject matter by means of our language? Since we simply do not have a word which adequately represents the biblical synthesis of the various meanings, I have frequently used words like communion or

Church, against which he wishes all future conceptions of the Church to be measured.[1] Naturally he does not do this in the form of a systematic treatise. What he does is to show us what, in essence, the Church is by illuminating the forward thrust of her path in history. This path begins with the sending of the Holy Spirit, who gives himself to a community united in prayer around Mary and the Apostles (Acts 1:12–14; 2:1).

If we consider this affirmation for a moment, we can see that it already highlights three of the Church's fundamental attributes, as they have been handed down to us. The Church is apostolic; she is a praying community, i.e., turned toward the Lord and therefore "holy"; and she is one. The first *sign* by which the Holy Spirit manifests his presence adds a fourth quality: the gift of languages. Thus he reverses the calamity of Babel. The new community, the new People of God, speaks in all languages and so, from the first moment of its existence, it is revealed as "catholic". The effects of the dynamism which lies in this sign, compelling the Church to go to the very ends of space and time—this is the

---

communio, to indicate at least the interconnected and related senses. I have to admit that I failed to find a completely satisfactory solution to the linguistic problem; it was not possible to avoid a certain arbitrariness in the choice of words. However, I trust that the context will make the reality clear enough. On all these issues, cf. J. Hainz, *Koinonia. "Kirche" als Gemeinschaft bei Paulus* (Regensburg 1982); P. C. Bori, κοινωνία *L'idea della communione nell'ecclesiologia recente e nel Nuove Testamento* (Brescia 1972); E. Kunz, "Eucharistie—Ursprung von Kommunikation und Gemeinschaft", in *TheolPhil* 58 (1983): 321–45.

[1] A helpful article on the basic stance of Acts is G. Schneider, "Apostelgeschichte und Kirchengeschichte", in *Internat. kath. Zeitschr. Communio* 8 (1979): 481–85; id., *Die Apostelgeschichte I* (Freiburg 1980), 134–54, which includes a generous bibliography.

theme of every chapter of the Acts of the Apostles, which describes the gospel's transition from the Jews to the Gentiles, from Jerusalem to Rome. In the structure of Acts, Rome, coming at the book's conclusion, stands for the Gentile world as a whole, the world of the nations, which was always seen in opposition to the ancient People of God. Acts ends with the arrival of the gospel in Rome—not as if the result of the court action against Paul were no longer of interest, but simply because the book is neither novel nor biography. Paul's arrival in Rome marks the goal of the path which began in Jerusalem; the universal—catholic—Church has been realized, in continuance of the ancient Chosen People and its history and taking over the latter's mission. Thus Rome, as a symbol for the world of the nations, has a theological status in Acts; it cannot be separated from the Lucan idea of catholicity.[2]

We could conclude this rough outline of Luke's ecclesiology by indicating a few characteristics of the Church as conceived by him. First of all, it is a pneumatological view of the Church, for it is the Spirit who creates the Church. It is a dynamic view of the Church's role in salvation history, in which the dimension of catholicity is essential. Finally, it is a liturgical eccle-

[2] The idea of Jerusalem being "translated" to Rome is presented in K. Hofstetter, "Das Petrusamt in der Kirche des 1.–2. Jhdts.: Jerusalem–Rom", in M. Roesle–O. Cullmann (ed.), *Begegnung der Christen*, 2nd ed. (Stuttgart 1960); cf. J. Ratzinger, *Das neue Volk Gottes* (Düsseldorf 1969), 128–31. An important book on this issue is V. Twomey, *Apostolikos Thronos: The primacy of Rome as reflected in the Church history of Eusebius and the historico-apologetic writings of St. Athanasius the Great* (Münster 1982). Twomey shows that the idea of the translation of Jerusalem to Rome is fundamental to the structure of Eusebius' Church history; it proves to be a very ancient tradition, which gradually fell into oblivion in the era of Constantine.

siology: the gathered community receives the gift of the Spirit in the act of prayer.

I. The Key: The Word κοινωνία (Fellowship)

1. The description of the Church in Acts 2:42

We have established that Luke describes the Church's essential dimensions by showing her pursuing her path, led by the Holy Spirit. But in the fabric of the Lucan text we can discern another thread which Luke has inserted in order to clarify the nature of the Church. In the picture of the primitive community he has sketched the exemplary form of the Church for all time. His vision of the Church is summed up in verse 42. Let us recall it: the first Christians, according to Acts, continued in "the Apostles' teaching and fellowship, the breaking of bread and the prayers". Here, therefore, we have four concepts adumbrating the Church's essence, and if we compare them with the account of Pentecost, we shall see that they correspond to, continue and deepen the latter's basic elements.[3]

Here, too, unity is a characteristic of the Church. Here too, unity arises out of fellowship with the apostles and from a turning to the living God in prayer. Now, however, this fellowship with the Apostles is defined more precisely thus: "They continued in the Apostles' *teaching*." That is, the unity has a content which is expressed in doctrine. The teaching of the Apostles is the concrete way in which they continue to be present in the Church.

---

[3] For the interpretation of this verse, cf. F. Mussner, "Die UNA SANCTA nach Apg. 2, 42", in id., *Praesentia salutis* (Düsseldorf 1967), 212–22.

In virtue of this teaching, even future generations, after the death of the Apostles, will remain in unity with them and thus form the same, one, apostolic Church. In order to get a better view of the way in which these things are linked, we must take into consideration Paul's farewell discourse to the presbyters of Ephesus, which is found in Acts 20:18–35. This is an exposition of what is meant by "apostolic teaching", for here Luke is developing the idea of apostolic discipleship. Now it appears that the teaching of the Apostles has a personal and an institutional aspect. The "presbyters" are entrusted with the responsibility of upholding the Apostles' teaching and ensuring that it remains a present reality. They are the personal guarantee for that "continung in" the original doctrine.[4]

Thus the idea of apostolicity is deepened and given concrete expression with a view to the Church having an abiding structure. Now a second aspect of the Church of Pentecost is expanded and clarified: the Church's "praying" finds its center of gravity in the "breaking of bread". The Eucharist reveals itself as the heart of Church life. But there is *one* concept, in this portrayal of the primitive Church—and hence of the Church of all times and places—which should be developed, namely, the word κοινωνία (*communicatio* in the Vulgate). This word, because of its wide range of meaning, must be the real key concept here, for it can mean "Eucharist" as well as "community" and "parish". It unites two realities which, in our language, can seem quite unrelated: Eucharist and community, that is, communion as sacrament and communion as a social and institutional reality.

This observation indicates the path for further reflection. First of all we need to follow the clue of κοινωνία in

[4] Cf. F. Mussner, 215f.; H. Schürmann, *Traditionsgeschichtliche Untersuchungen zu den synoptischen Evangelien* (Düsseldorf 1967), 310–40.

its various associations, so that this concept may throw light on the relationship between Eucharist and community, or rather, on the eucharistic dynamism of community within the Church. Then we shall take our reflections a stage further and consider the figure of Jesus Christ, in an attempt to find in him, the origin and center of Christian communio, a spirituality of "communicating" which would also be available to those who cannot share in the narrower sacramental communion. When Christians speak of "communicating", they are not referring to something which characterizes and circumscribes one group of people: because of its christological basis, this "communicating" always means mission too, it means acting on behalf of the others who are still "outside", approaching them. This is, of course, a very rudimentary outline; we cannot go into details here. The present aim is to underline certain essential features of the Catholic tradition and to stimulate further thought.

2. The legal, sacramental and practical content of the word communio in Acts 2:42 and Galations 2:9–10

Before pursuing this examination, let us briefly recapitulate our analysis of Acts 2:42. So far, we have simply established in general that the word κοινωνία, with its wide range of meaning, plays an important role in the portrayal of the Church's essence. We have yet to ask what precisely it means in this particular verse. The answers of the biblical scholars differ, and the context itself scarcely warrants an indisputable decision. Two things, however, can be said. The word stands between the two concepts "teaching" and "breaking of bread" (Eucharist); in some respect it seems to be a bridge linking the two. Moreover, Luke gives us the four words in two pairs: "teaching and fellowship", "breaking of bread and the prayers". Thus fellowship is linked with "apostolic teaching" and forms, as it were, a solid unity with it and is to that extent distinct from the breaking of bread (Eucharist); at all events it is portrayed as something going beyond the practice of worship, something essentially rooted in the fundamental fact of constantly maintained tradition and its ecclesial form.

This initially somewhat surprising aspect confronts us even more strongly and clearly in Paul's self-defense in the Letter to the Galatians, where he presents both the authorization of his own mission and also his basic view of ecclesial community (Gal 1:13–2:14). In that part of the text which interests us here, Paul records that the so-called "pillars of the Church"—James, Peter and John—gave "the right hand of fellowship" (κοινωίας, *societatis* in the Vulgate) to him and to Barnabas.[5] These three "pillars" were apparently the continuation, in the primitive Church, of the group of three Apostles whom Jesus had chosen as the innermost core of the Twelve and admitted to the event of his Transfiguration and to his mortal agony in Gethsemane (cf. Mk 9:2; 14:33; cf. also Mk 5:37). Evidently these "pillars" were responsible for leading the growing Church; they decided who should be admitted or excluded.[6] In giving Paul and Barnabas

---

[5] Cf. H. Schlier, *Der Brief an die Galater* (Göttingen 1962), 78–81; F. Mussner, *Der Galaterbrief* (Freiburg 1974), 115–27, 423; id., " 'Das Wesen des Christentums ist συνεσθίειν'. Ein authentischer Kommentar", in H. Rossmann–J. Ratzinger, *Mysterium der Gnade. Festschrift für J. Auer* (Regensburg 1975), 92–102.

[6] The Qumran community was also aware of the distinction between the Three and the Twelve and of the symbolism involved. On the relation and distinction of the two groupings within the structure of Jesus' community of disciples, cf. A. Vögtle, *Das öffentliche Wirken Jesu auf dem Hintergrund der Qumranbewegung* (Freiburger

the right to communio, they were performing an authoritative and binding declaration of ecclesial fellowship—an act which even Paul regarded as indispensable, however much he stressed that he was called directly by the Lord and received direct revelation. For Paul too, the unity of the Church is unthinkable apart from this "continuing in the teaching of the Apostles", i.e., in the Church's apostolic structure. Accordingly, the word "communio" here has its full Christian significance, embracing the sacramental and spiritual as well as the institutional and personal dimensions. This "right hand of fellowship", imparted at the so-called Council of Jerusalem which is reported in Acts 15:1–35, authorized the path taken by Paul and Barnabas in promoting a Gentile Church free from the Jewish law; it actually established ecclesial communio, in the real sense, for the first time, i.e., the new People, composed of Jews and Gentiles, both taken up into the open arms of the crucified Christ (cf. Jn 12:32).

The succeeding passage from Paul's self-defense shows, however, how hard it was to do justice to the implications of this decision and thus reveals how profound a decision it was. For, in spite of the clarification achieved, the question of dietary prescriptions in Antioch almost opened up a rift again. The issue had rendered table fellowship impossible between the two groups; they could not eat the same things, and so they could not eat together, because the Christians who came from Judaism

---

Universitätsreden 1958), 15f.; F. Nötscher, "Vorchristliche Typen urchristlicher Ämter? Episkopos und Mebagger", in Corsten "Frotz" Linden, *Die Kirche und ihre Ämter und Stände* (Cologne 1958), 315–38, esp. 328f. It seems worthy of note that, even after the death of James the son of Zebedee, the Church maintained the group of Three which the Lord had created by putting James the Lord's brother in the place of the deceased James.

regarded the dietary prescriptions, which were at the heart of their religious observance, as indispensable, whereas the Gentile Christians felt in no way bound by them. A split in "secular" table fellowship (though, for Jewish Christians keeping the law, such fellowship was never something purely "secular") inevitably resulted in dissolving the fellowship of the Lord's Supper. So they were faced once more with the question, in even sharper focus, which had been at issue in the fundamental agreement on communio at the Council of Jerusalem: either the Church became a Jewish sect, of which there were many, or she allowed herself to be cut off from her root, the Old Testament—the very Old Testament which provided her legitimacy as a religion of revelation. For it is impossible to have the Son without the Father, impossible to have Jesus without his Bible, which we call the Old Testament. Marcion tried to do this in the second century in his program of radicalized Paulinism, and his followers have kept on trying to do it ever since (including some modern theologians); but the attempt is self-contradictory and doomed to failure. If we go back to the "right hand of fellowship" in Jerusalem, what it means is that, in Jesus, in whom the law is fulfilled, we possess the Old Testament. It means that faith in Christ, and it alone, establishes communion. When Paul so strongly reminds the "pillars"—i.e., Peter, to put it quite concretely—of the communio agreed at Jerusalem, he shows, through his vehement insistence, that it is essential to have the concrete sign of valid unity, the "continuing in the teaching of the Apostles", if one is to abide in unity with the crucified and risen Lord.

However, we must return to the account of the crucial Jerusalem decision in order to focus on another aspect of communio, which again involves both visible, "institutional" fellowship and the spiritual dimension of Christian existence. Paul emphasizes that they have accepted that Gentile Christians (and hence all Christians) are completely free from the law, without any reservations. There was one injunction laid upon the Gentile Christians, but it was of a totally different kind, namely, to be solicitous for the "poor" of Jerusalem. What does this mean? First of all I think we must stress the social character of this injunction: fellowship in and with the Body of Christ means fellowship with one another. Of its very essence, it implies mutual acceptance, give and take and the readiness to share. Where fellowship in the Church is concerned, it should be impossible for some to enjoy luxury while others lack bare necessities. Fellowship in the Church is always "table fellowship" in the fullest sense; the Church's members are pledged to give "life" to one another, spiritual *and* physical life. In this sense, the social question is at the theological core of the Christian concept of communio.

However, there is a further aspect. The "poor" of whom this passage speaks are not only (and not even primarily) a social group; the term is also a messianic title applied to the Jerusalem community, like the appellation "the saints". So the collection of alms for the "poor" is at the same time an acknowledgment of the importance of Jerusalem in saving history, as the initial locus of unity and focus of the history of salvation.[7] It expresses the

[7] Thus, e.g., H. O. Wendland, "Geist, Recht und Amt in der Urkirche", in *Arch. Ev. Kirchenrecht*, new series, 2 (1938): 299. H. Schlier, 80f. (cf. note 5) also shows that the collection for the Jerusalem "poor" was intended less to relieve those in distress than to encourage a recognition of the primacy of Jerusalem and an awareness of the Church's unity. It must be noted that Schlier stresses that the primacy was a moral and religious, not a juridical, primacy. This

primacy of Jerusalem at a time when, for Christians, Jerusalem was still the center and the translation to Rome had not yet taken place. The "Jerusalem" theme, with its implicit idea of primacy, is thus part and parcel of embryonic communio; it establishes a concrete standard for "continuing in the Apostles' teaching". This one text, therefore, reveals the various levels of the *communio christiana*, which are all ultimately rooted in one and the same thing, namely, fellowship with the incarnate Word of God, who, through his death, enables us to share in his life. Thus too he wishes to lead us to minister to one another, to partake in a visible and lived fellowship.

3. The secular roots of the concept κοινωνία and what they imply in terms of the new Christian reality

a. The transformation of the secular meaning in Luke's Gospel

Human words, at least the great fundamental words, always carry with them a whole history of human experiences, human questionings, understandings and the sufferings wrought by reality. The great watchwords of the Bible draw mankind's basic experience, in acceptance and rejection, into the process of revelation. In order to understand the Bible properly, therefore, we must always go back to the historical experience preserved in its words. With this in mind, let us endeavor to appreciate the historical burden of the concept of κοινωνία.

---

distinction only applies if one assumes a modern, restricted concept of what is moral and what is juridical. While this modern concept accords with our way of speaking and thinking, it is inappropriate to the governing perspectives of that period.

We discern an initial, secular significance of the word in a passage in Luke's Gospel which illuminates the beginnings of the reality which we call Church. I refer to the first eleven verses of chapter 5, where the Evangelist narrates the calling of the first disciples in a scene of incomparable beauty. After a night in which the fishermen had toiled in vain on the Lake of Gennesareth, the new morning dawns together with the dawning Gospel, and the Lord bestows on them a superabundant catch of fish and calls Peter and his companions to become fishers of men. In the Fourth Gospel this scene will be repeated after the Resurrection (Jn 21:1–14)—after Peter's denial, and then it will contain a definitive mission to go out onto the vast ocean of the whole world.

I think it very significant that our word occurs in this scene of Luke's, which is like a vision of what is to come: James and John are referred to as κοινωνοί of Simon (v. 10), which is translated inadequately as "partners" —obliterating the associations of the word which particularly interest us. The three men, whose fellowship (as we saw) will be continued in the "pillars" of the Letter to the Galatians, are there at the beginning of Jesus' public ministry and form a "commune". It is clear that the word at this point has no theological connotation; it is used as a generally current term for fellow tradesmen. James and John are Simon's "associates", "partners" in fishing; the three of them are in "partnership". They are joint owners of a small business, with Simon in overall charge.[8] Here, then, is the original, secular sense of the word, which will remain important for an understanding of its new religious sense: κοινωνία implies common

[8] Cf. J. Hamer, *L'Église est une communion* (Paris 1962), 176; F. Hauck, κοινωνία in *ThWNT* 4:804; H. Schürmann, *Das Lukasevangelium I* (Freiburg 1969), 270f.

property, working together, shared values. In Jesus' "Henceforth you will be catching men", Simon's erstwhile trade becomes an allegory of his future vocation. Similarly the fishing partnership becomes a sign of the new "partnership", the new communio. Christians will be the "company of the tiny bark of the Church", one in their calling by Jesus, one by the miracle of grace which harvests the wealth of the sea after nights of hopelessness. Since they are one in grace, they will also be one in their mission, which is itself grace.

The ancient Church, in reflecting on this text, recognized what constitutes the deep foundations of the unity of this "partnership": what makes it one is ultimately the mysterious fish, the Risen Lord, who descended into the depths of the sea—the night of death—and let himself be caught by us and for us, to become our food for eternal life. We are the bark of Peter, and thus we are those called by the Lord; we are partners of Peter, we are not the company of Peter, however, but the communio of the Lord himself, who bestows on us what we ourselves could never achieve. What we receive comes before what we do, or, as J. Hamer puts it: in communion (κοινωνία) the horizontal dimension depends on the vertical and can only be understood on that basis.[9]

b. Jewish roots

As we would expect, the word of the Greek New Testament which we are trying to understand has a Hebrew root. The Hebrew word *ḥabhûrâ* corresponds to the Greek κοινωνία and, like the latter, designates a

[9] Hamer, 1976.

partnership, a "cooperative". Naturally, the specific conditions of Hebrew society are reflected in the word and impart a particular coloration to the way it is used. Three aspects present themselves. As early as the first century B.C. the group of the Pharisees call themselves *ḥabhûrâ*; since the second century A.D. the term is also used for the rabbis; and ultimately the word is applied to those (at least ten in number) assembled for the Passover meal.[10] This latter usage shows quite clearly how easily it could be applied to the mystery of the Church: the Church is the *ḥabhûrâ* of Jesus in a very deep sense—the fellowship of his Passover, the family in which his eternal desire of eating the Passover with us (cf. Lk 24:15) is fulfilled. But this Passover of his is far more than a meal: it is a love which goes as far as death. Thus it gives us a share, a participation, in his own life, which, in death, is divided up among us all. His life communicates itself in a voluntary anticipation of death in the words, "Take, eat, this is my body which is given for you. Take and drink ye all of this; this is the cup of my blood which is shed for many."

Here, in unique clarity, we come to what is specific to the New Testament, to what makes it new as opposed to the history of the Covenant up to that time—which thus becomes the "Old" Testament. In the Old Testament, too, sacrifice and the sacrificial meal are designed to create a communion between God and his people. But the word *ḥabhûrâ*—communio—is never used to designate the relationship between God and man; it is used exclusively to refer to relations between men. Between God and man there can be no "communio"; the Creator's transcendence remains an impassable barrier. Consequently the concrete

[10] Hauck, 802f. Cf. the essay "The Passover of Jesus and the Church" in this volume.

relation between God and man which is essential for the Old Testament is not given the word "communion" but the word "covenant" (*berith*).[11] This terminology safeguards God's sublime majesty (for he alone can determine what relationship the creature may enter into with him), and hence it also establishes the distance which remains between the two. Because of this, many Scripture scholars hold it to be wrong to translate *berith* as "covenant", since the latter implies a certain equality of the covenant "partners", which, in the Old Testament view, is impossible in the God-man relationship. We need not pursue this question here; what is important for us is the fact that the Old Testament knows of no "communion" (*ḥabhûrâ*, κοινωνία) between God and man; the New Testament *is* this communion, in and through the Person of Jesus Christ.

c. The Greek background and the problem of the Hellenization of Christianity

A third element is contributed to the Christian word by Greek philosophy, which, as we shall see, views things in a way fundamentally opposed to the mode of thought of the Hebrew Bible. So the particular issue which concerns us will also shed light on the much-discussed question of the "Hellenization" of Christianity.

The Old Testament opposes pagan polytheism to the transcendence and unity of God. We have just seen that this results in a rejection of the idea that God and man can actually "commune" with each other. For the pagan world, however, it is this very idea which is at the center

---

[11] Hauck, 801f.

of the religious search. Thus Plato speaks of the reciprocal communion between the gods and men (ἡ περὶ θεοὺς καὶ ἀνθρώπους κοινωνία). According to him, communion with the gods also brings about community among men. He asserts that this communion is the ultimate aim, the deepest meaning, of all sacrifice and of all cultic activity whatsoever. In this connection he coins a wonderful phrase, which could actually be taken as an intimation of the eucharistic mystery, when he says that the cult is concerned with nothing other than the preservation and the healing of love.[12] It must be added that communion between Divinity, man and all rational beings is a central idea in Hellenistic mysticism. But the real aim of this mysticism is not communion but union; its ultimate goal is not relationship but identity.[13] When Philo distances himself from the traditional Hebrew terminology and speaks of "communion" between God and the believer in the cult, in the terms of Hellenistic mysticism, there may be a certain justification for speaking of a "Hellenization" of Hebrew thought. But it is quite different in the New Testament, where the Church *is* communion— communion not only between human beings but, as a result of the death and Resurrection of Jesus, communion with Christ, the incarnate Son, and hence communion with the eternal, triune Love of God. For this is not the product of a new synthesis of *thought*, but the fruit of a new *reality* which was previously nonexistent. The one, transcendent God of the Old Testament unveils his inner-most life and shows that, in himself, he is a dialogue of eternal love. Since he himself is relationship—Word and Love—he can speak, feel, answer, love. Since he is

---

[12] *Symposion* 188 b-c: . . . οὐπερὶ ἄλλο τι ἐστὶν ἢ περῖ Ερωτος φυλακήν τε καὶ ἴασιν. Cf. Hauck, 800.
[13] Ibid.

relationship, he can open himself and provide his creature with a relationship to him. In the Incarnation of the eternal Word there comes about that communion between God and the being of man, his creature, which up to now had seemed irreconcilable with the transcendence of the only God.

Plato's observation that cultic activity is concerned with communion between the gods and man's being, in order to maintain love and to activate its healing power, now acquires new significance. Let us take note that Plato speaks, not of God, but of the gods, and that Hellenistic mysticism prefers to speak of the Divinity rather than of God. In Jesus, however, a new event takes place, in that the only God actually and really enters into communion with men by taking flesh in human nature. Divine and human nature interpenetrate—"without confusion, without separation"—in the Person of Jesus Christ. Obviously it would be absurd to speak of "Hellenization" of the Christian phenomenon at this point and to call for a return to the pure, Hebraic origin. This would mean abandoning what is specifically Christian, the new Christian reality. In fact, the Incarnation is the new synthesis performed by God himself. Of necessity, it oversteps the boundary of the Old Testament as it gathers up and safeguards the latter's full inheritance, in order to open it up and enrich it with the wealth of the other cultures. For Incarnation is also the reconciliation, the bringing into fellowship (communio) of those who were formerly at odds—Jews and Gentiles (cf. Eph 2:11–22); this also applies to the realm of thought. The purists who accuse us of Hellenization, and who want to return to the plain Hebraic view, simply demonstrate that they are blind to the nature of Christianity.

II. Eucharist, Christology, Ecclesiology: The Christological Core

1. Eucharist and Christology

Our analysis of the inner development of the Christian concept of communio, in its role of gathering up and refashioning the pre-Christian inheritance, has quite naturally led us to the heart of what is meant by Christian communio. We are now in a position to say that its source lies in Christology: the incarnate Son is the "communion" between God and men. Being a Christian is in reality nothing other than sharing in the mystery of the Incarnation, or as St. Paul puts it: the Church, insofar as she is the Church, is the "Body of Christ" (i.e., a participation on the part of men in that communion between man and God which is the Incarnation of the Word). Once this has been grasped, it is clear that there can be no separation of Church and Eucharist, sacramental communion and community fellowship.

These insights also illuminate those fundamental words of St. Paul on our topic which are to be found in the first Letter to the Corinthians: "The cup of blessing which we bless, is it not a participation (κοινωνία, communicatio in the Vulgate) in the blood of Christ? The bread which we break, is it not a participation (κοινωνία, participatio in the Vulgate; communicatio in the Neo-Vulgate) in the body of Christ? Because there is one bread, we who are many are one body, for we all partake of the one bread" (1 Cor 10:16ff.). These words became the core of Augustine's theological thought; his homilies for the Easter Vigil, which were his catechesis on the Eucharist for the newly baptized, circle around them. By eating the one bread, he says, we ourselves become what we eat.[14] In the Confessions he says that this bread is nourishment for the strong.[15] Normal food is less strong than man, it serves him, is taken into man's body to be assimilated and to build it up. But this special food, the Eucharist, is above man and stronger than man. Consequently the whole process involved is reversed: the man who eats this bread is assimilated *by it*, taken into it; he is fused into this bread and becomes bread, like Christ himself. "Though many, we are one body, for we are one bread." The result of this insight is quite clear: Eucharist is never merely an event à *deux*, a dialogue between Christ and me. The goal of eucharistic communion is a total recasting of a person's life, breaking up a man's whole "I" and creating a new "We". Communion with Christ is of necessity a communication with all those who are his: it means that I myself become part of this new "bread" which he creates by transubstantiating all earthly reality.

Here we glimpse the close connection which exists between the concept of communio and our understanding of the Church as the "Body of Christ". Here too is the context for related images, such as Christ as the true Vine. All these biblical ideas again shed light on the fact that Christian fellowship comes from Christ. The Christian "community" cannot be explained in a merely horizontal, essentially sociological manner. Its existence presupposes this relationship to the Lord as its origin and goal. Indeed, we can say that the Church, of her essence, is relationship, a relationship created by the love of

[14] Cf. J. Ratzinger, *Volk und Haus Gottes in Augustins Lehre von der Kirche* (Munich 1954).
[15] *Conf.* VII 10, 16.

Christ, and she in turn founds a new relationship between men. We can echo those beautiful words of Plato and say that the Eucharist is in fact the "healing of our love".

2. The communion of divinity and humanity in Christ

Now we must take a second step and define even more clearly the christological foundation of Christian existence. Thus we shall draw closer to both the core of eucharistic spirituality and the core of a spirituality of the Church. As we have seen in our reflections so far, Jesus Christ opens the way to the impossible, to communion between God and man, since he, the incarnate Word, is this communion. He performs the "alchemy" which melts down human nature and infuses it into the being of God. To receive the Lord in the Eucharist, therefore, means entering into a community of being with Christ, it means entering through that opening in human nature through which God is accessible—which is the precondition for human beings opening up to one another in a really deep way. Communion with God is the path to interpersonal communion among men. If we are to grasp the spiritual content of the Eucharist, therefore, we must understand the spiritual tension which marks the God-man: only in the context of a spiritual Christology will the spirituality of the sacrament reveal itself to us.

Western theology, with its predominantly metaphysical and historical concerns, has rather neglected this aspect, which is in fact the link between the various disciplines of theology and between theological reflection and the concrete, spiritual working out of Christianity. The Third Council of Constantinople (the thirteen hundredth anniversary of which, in 1981, was—significantly enough—almost forgotten, compared with the celebrations commemorating the First Council of Constantinople and that of Ephesus) sets forth the essential elements which, in my view, are also fundamental to a proper interpretation of the Council of Chalcedon. Obviously, we do not have space to make a thorough exposition of the problems, but let us at least try briefly to outline the issues which concern us here.[16] Chalcedon had described the ontological content of the Incarnation with its celebrated formula of Two Natures in One Person. This ontology signaled the beginning of a great dispute, and the Third Council of Constantinople found itself confronted with the question: What is the spiritual substance of this ontology? Or, more concretely: What does it mean, in practical and existential terms, to speak of "One Person in Two Natures"? How can a person live with two wills and a twofold intellect? These were by no means questions posed out of theoretical curiosity; the questions affect us too, for the issue is this: How can *we* live as baptized people, to whom Paul's words must apply: "I live, yet not I, but Christ liveth in me" (Gal 2:20)?

As is well known, then—in the seventh century—as today, two solutions which were equally unacceptable presented themselves. Some said that in Christ there was in fact no actual human will. The Third Council of Constantinople rejects this picture of Christ as that of a "Christ lacking in both will and power". The other solution took the opposite view and assumed that there were two completely separate spheres of will in Christ. But this led to a kind of schizophrenia, a monstrous suggestion which was also unacceptable. The Council's

[16] Text in *Conciliorum oecumenicorum decreta*, ed. Alberigo et al., 3d ed. (Bologna 1973), 124–30; cf. Thesis 6 of "Taking Bearings in Christology" in this volume.

answer is this: the ontological *union* of two faculties of will which remain independent within the unity of the Person means that, at the existential level, there is a *communion* (κοινωνία) of the two wills. With this interpretation of union as communion, the Council sketches an ontology of freedom. The two "wills" are united in the way in which two wills can be united, namely, in a common affirmation of a shared value. In other words, what unites the two wills is the Yes of Christ's human will to the divine will of the Logos. Thus, in concrete terms—"existentially"—the two wills become a single will while remaining, at the ontological level, two independent realities. The Council adds that, just as the Lord's flesh may be called the flesh of the Logos, his human will may also be termed the Logos' own will. In practice the Council is here applying the trinitarian model (with the mandatory ever-greater difference in the analogy) to Christology: the highest unity there is—the unity of God—is not the unity of unstructured, amorphous substance but unity by communion, a unity which both creates and is love. Thus the Logos adopts the being of the man Jesus into his own being and speaks of it in terms of his own I: "For I have come down from heaven, not to do my own will, but the will of him who sent me" (Jn 6:38).[17] In the Son's obedience, where both wills become one in a single Yes to the will of the Father, communion takes place between human and divine being. The "wondrous exchange", the "alchemy of being", is realized here as a liberating and reconciling communication, which becomes a communion between Creator and creature. It is in the pain of this exchange, and only here, that that fundamental change takes place in man,

[17] *Conciliorum oecumenicorum decreta* 128, 130ff.

the change which alone can redeem him and transform the conditions of the world. Here community is born, here the Church comes into being. The act whereby we participate in the Son's obedience, which involves man's genuine transformation, is also the only really effective contribution toward renewing and transforming society and the world as a whole. Only where this act takes place is there a change for good—in the direction of the kingdom of God.[18]

I offer a further consideration for the sake of completeness. We have established that the Incarnation of the Son creates communion between God and man and thus also makes possible a new communion among human beings. This communion between God and man, which is realized in the Person of Jesus Christ, itself becomes communicable in the Easter mystery, i.e., in the Lord's death and Resurrection. The Eucharist is our participation in the Easter mystery, and hence it is constitutive of the Church, the Body of Christ. This is why the Eucharist is necessary for salvation. The necessity of the Eucharist is identical with the necessity of the Church and vice versa. This is how we should understand the Lord's saying: "Unless you eat the flesh of the Son of man and drink his blood, you have no life in you" (Jn 6:53). Hence we see the necessity, too, of a visible Church and a visible, concrete (and one might say "institutional") unity. The most

[18] It was Maximus the Confessor who explored theologically the Third Council of Constantinople; cf. F.-M. Lethel, *Théologie de l'agonie du Christ* (Paris 1979); F. Heinzer, *Gottes Sohn als Mensch. Die Struktur des Menschseins Christi bei Maximus Confessor* (Fribourg 1980); K. H. Uthemann, "Das anthropologische Modell der hypostatischen Union bei Maximus Confessor. Zur innerchalkedonischen Transformation eines Paradigmas", in F. Heinzer–Chr. Schönborn (ed.), *Maximus Confessor* (Fribourg 1982), 223–33; L. Weimer, *Die Lust an Gott und seiner Sache* (Freiburg 1981), 101–6.

intimate mystery of communion between God and man is accessible in the sacrament of the *Body* of the Risen Lord; conversely, then, the mystery lays claim to our *bodies* and is realized in a *Body*. The Church, which is built upon the sacrament of the Body of Christ, must herself be a body. And she must be a single body, corresponding to Jesus Christ's uniqueness, a uniqueness which is reflected in unity and in the "continuing in" the one, apostolic teaching.

3. The problem of the excommunicate

If this is how things are, what are we to say of the many Christians who believe and hope in the Lord, who yearn for the gift of his body but cannot receive the sacrament? People are excluded from sacramental communion in very different ways. First of all there are those who are simply unable to receive the sacrament in time of persecution or as a result of a lack of priests. Then there are those who are excluded from communion on judicial grounds, like the divorced and remarried. The question also touches on the ecumenical problem of the lack of communio among separated Christians. Of course we cannot deal with such diverse and extensive issues here, but it would be a failure in sincerity if we simply ignored them. While an answer is impossible in the present work, I would like at least to mention one important aspect. In his book *L'Église est une communion*, J. Hamer shows that medieval theology too could not avoid the problem of excommunication and dealt with it, in fact, most conscientiously. Medieval thinkers were no longer able—unlike the Fathers—simply to equate membership of the Church's visible communion with a relationship to the Lord. Gratian could write: Beloved, a Christian who is excluded from communion by the priests has been consigned to the devil. Why? Because outside the Church there is the devil, whereas within the Church there is Christ.[19] By contrast, the theologians of the thirteenth century were faced with a twofold task: on the one hand, they were bound to preserve the link between the internal and the external, between sign and reality, body and spirit, and at the same time they had to do justice to the distinction between them. Thus, for instance, William of Auvergne observes that exterior and interior communion are linked like sign and reality. He goes on to say that the Church never wishes to deprive anyone of interior communion. When she wields the sword of excommunication, it is solely for the purpose of applying medicaments to this spiritual communion. And he adds a thought which is both consoling and stimulating: he is aware, he says, that, for not a few, the burden of excommunication is as hard to bear as martyrdom. But it sometimes happens that such an excommunicate person progresses further along the path of patience and humility than if he were able to receive communion.[20] Bonaventure developed this idea. He discovered a very modern-sounding objection to the Church's right to exclude people: Excommunication is separation from communion. But Christian communion, of its essence, exists through love; it is a fellowship of love. And since no one has the right to exclude anyone from love, neither can there be a right to excommunicate anyone.[21] Bonaventure answers by distinguishing three

[19] Hamer, 184; *Decr. Grat.* C XI q 3 c 32.
[20] *De sacramento Ordinis* cap. 12 (Venice 1591), 519 A–C; cf. Hamer, 187.
[21] *IV Sent* d 18 p 2 a un q 1 contr 1; Hamer, 187f.

levels of communion; this enables him to hold fast to Church discipline and Church law, while maintaining, as a responsible theologian: "I assert that no one can be, and no one may be, excluded from the communion of love as long as he lives on earth. Excommunication is not such an exclusion."[22]

Such reflections, which need to be taken up and developed today, must not, of course, be used to substantiate the idea that actual, sacramental communion is superfluous or less important. For the "ex-communicate" is supported by the love of the living Body of Christ, by the sufferings of the saints, who unite with his suffering and his spiritual hunger, and both parties are enveloped by the suffering, the hunger, the thirst of Jesus Christ, who bears and endures us all. On the other hand, the suffering of the excommunicate person, his stretching out for communion (the communion of the sacrament and of the living members of Christ) is the bond which unites him to the saving love of Christ. Thus, from both sides, the sacrament and the visible communion which it builds and nourishes are both present and indispensable. Here too, therefore, the "healing of love" takes place, which is the ultimate aim of Christ's Cross, of the sacrament and of the Church. We can understand how, paradoxically, the impossibility of sacramental communion, experienced in a sense of remoteness from God, in the pain of yearning which fosters the growth of love, can lead to spiritual progress, whereas rebellion—as William of Auvergne rightly says—inevitably destroys the positive and constructive sense of excommunication. Rebellion is not the healing but the destroying of love.

Here I am struck by a consideration of a more general

[22] Ibid., ad 1; Hamer, 188.

and pastoral kind. When Augustine sensed his death approaching, he "excommunicated" himself and undertook public penance. In his last days he manifested his solidarity with the public sinners who seek for pardon and grace through the renunciation of communion.[23] He wanted to meet his Lord in the humility of those who hunger and thirst for righteousness, for him who is the Righteous and Merciful One. Against the background of his sermons and writings, which are a magnificent portrayal of the mystery of the Church as communion with the Body of Christ, and as the Body of Christ itself, built up by the Eucharist, this is a profoundly arresting gesture. The more I think of it, the more it moves me to reflection. Do we not often take the reception of the Blessed Sacrament too lightly? Might not this kind of spiritual fasting be of service, or even necessary, to deepen and renew our relationship to the Body of Christ?

The ancient Church had a highly expressive practice of this kind. Since apostolic times, no doubt, the fast from the Eucharist on Good Friday was a part of the Church's spirituality of communion. This renunciation of communion on one of the most sacred days of the Church's year was a particularly profound way of sharing in the Lord's Passion; it was the Bride's mourning for the lost Bridegroom (cf. Mk 2:20).[24] Today too, I think, fasting from the Eucharist, really taken seriously and entered into, could be most meaningful on carefully considered

[23] Cf. J. van der Meer, *Augustinus der Seelsorger* (Cologne 1951), 324.

[24] On the question of Christian fasting, in connection with Mark 2:20, cf. R. Pesch, *Das Markusevangelium I* (Freiburg 1976), 175f.; on the problem of the eucharistic fast, motivated by considerations of eschatology; J. Blank, *Meliton von Sardes. Vom Passa. Die älteste christliche Osterpredigt* (Freiburg 1963), 26–41.

occasions, such as days of penance—and why not reintroduce the practice on Good Friday? It would be particularly appropriate at Masses where there is a vast congregation, making it impossible to provide for a dignified distribution of the sacrament; in such cases the renunciation of the sacrament could in fact express more reverence and love than a reception which does not do justice to the immense significance of what is taking place. A fasting of this kind—and of course it would have to be open to the Church's guidance and not arbitrary—could lead to a deepening of personal relationship with the Lord in the sacrament. It could also be an act of solidarity with all those who yearn for the sacrament but cannot receive it. It seems to me that the problem of the divorced and remarried, as well as that of intercommunion (e.g., in mixed marriages), would be far less acute against the background of voluntary spiritual fasting, which would visibly express the fact that we all need that "healing of love" which the Lord performed in the ultimate loneliness of the Cross. Naturally, I am not suggesting a return to a kind of Jansenism: fasting presupposes normal eating, both in spiritual and biological life. But from time to time we do need a medicine to stop us from falling into mere routine which lacks all spiritual dimension. Sometimes we need hunger, physical and spiritual hunger, if we are to come fresh to the Lord's gifts and understand the suffering of our hungering brothers. Both spiritual and physical hunger can be a vehicle of love.

Conclusion

Let us sum up what has been said and make a final observation. The biblical and patristic word κοινωνία unites in itself the two meanings "Eucharist" and "community" (fellowship). With this semantic synthesis it not only points to the heart of all ecclesiology, properly understood; it also indicates that necessary synthesis of the particular church and the universal Church. For the eucharistic celebration takes place in a particular place and builds there a cell of Christian brotherhood. The local "parish community" is nourished by the living and effectual presence of the Lord in the Eucharist. But at the same time it is true that it is the same Lord, the one Lord, in all places and in every Eucharist. So the indivisible presence of one and the same Lord, who is also the Father's Word, presupposes that every individual community is part of the entire, single Body of Christ. This is the only way the community can celebrate Eucharist at all. As we have seen, it also presupposes that it is "continuing in the teaching of the Apostles", something manifested and guaranteed by the institution of the "apostolic succession". Outside this vast net, "community" becomes empty, a romantic gesture of longing for security in a small group, which, however, lacks content.[25] It takes a power and a love which is stronger than all our own initiatives to build fruitful and dependable community and to equip it with the dynamism of a fruitful vocation. The unity of the Church, which is founded on the love of the one Lord, does not destroy what is distinctive of the individual communities but builds them up and maintains them as a

[25] On these questions, cf. J. Ratzinger, *Theologische Prinzipienlehre* (Munich 1982), 300–314.

real communion with the Lord and with one another. The love of Christ, which is present for all times in the sacrament of his Body, arouses our love, heals our love. The Eucharist is the foundation, day by day, of both community and vocation.

Part Two

Three Meditations

The Passover of Jesus and the Church

A Meditation for Holy Thursday

Israel's Passover was and is a family celebration.[1] It was celebrated in the home, not in the Temple. In the history of the foundation of the People of Israel, in Exodus (12:1–14), it is the home which is the locus of salvation and refuge in that night of darkness in which the Angel of Death walked abroad. For Egypt, in contrast, that night spelled the power of death, of destruction, of chaos, things that continually rise up from the deep places of the world and of man, threatening to wreck the good creation and reduce the world to an uninhabitable wilderness. In this situation it is the home, the family, which provides protection; in other words, the world always needs to be defended against chaos, creation always needs shielding and recreating. In the calendar of the nomads from whom Israel adopted the Passover festival, Passover was New Year's Day, i.e., the day on which the creation was refounded, when it had to be defended once again against the inroads of the void. The home, the family, is life's protective rampart, the place

This is a slightly edited version of a sermon I delivered on Holy Thursday 1981 in the Liebfrauendom in Munich. I have deliberately retained the character of the spoken word.

[1] The historical material in this sermon comes from H. Gese, "Die Herkunft des Herrenmahls", in H. Gese, *Zur biblischen Theologie* (Munich 1977), 107–27, esp. 111 with its important note 5. Cf. also in this volume the chapter "Communion, Community and Mission", I 3 b.

of security, of "shalom", of that peace and togetherness which lives and lets live, which holds the world together.

In the time of Jesus, too, Passover was celebrated in the homes and in families, following the slaughter of the lambs in the Temple. A regulation forbade anyone to leave the city of Jerusalem in the night of the Passover. The entire city was felt to be the locus of salvation over against the chaotic night, its walls the rampart protecting the creation. Israel had to make a pilgrimage, as it were, to the city every year at Passover in order to return to its origins, to be recreated and to experience once again its rescue, liberation and foundation. A very deep insight lies behind this. In the course of a year, a people is always in danger of disintegrating, not only through external causes, but also interiorly, and of losing hold of the inner motivation which sustains it. It needs to return to its fundamental origin. Passover was intended to be this annual event in which Israel returned from the threatening chaos (which lurks in every people) to its sustaining origin; it was meant to be the renewed defense and recreation of Israel in the basis of its origin. And since Israel knew that the star of its election stood in the heavens, it also knew that its fortunes, for good or ill, had consequences for the whole world; it knew that the destiny of the earth and of creation was involved in its response, whether it failed or passed the test.

Jesus too celebrated the Passover according to these prescriptions, at home with his family; that is to say, with the Apostles, who had become his new family. In doing so he was observing a current rule which permitted pilgrims who were traveling to Jerusalem to form companies, the so-called *ḥabhûroth*, who would constitute a family, a Passover unit, for this night. That is how Passover became a Christian feast. We are Christ's *ḥabhûrâ*, his family, formed of his pilgrim company, of the friends who accompany him along the path of the gospel through the terrain of history. Companions of his pilgrimage, we constitute Christ's house; thus, the Church is the new family, the new city, and for us she signifies all that Jerusalem was—that living home which banishes the powers of chaos and makes an area of peace, which upholds both creation and *us*. The Church is the new city by being the family of Jesus, the living Jerusalem, and her faith is the rampart and wall against the chaotic powers that threaten to bring destruction upon the world. Her ramparts are strengthened by the blood of the true Lamb, Jesus Christ, that is, by love which goes to the very end and which is endless. It is this love which is the true counterforce to chaos: it is the creative power which continually establishes the world afresh, providing new foundations for peoples and families, thus giving *us* "shalom", the realm of peace in which we can live with, for and unto one another. There are many reasons, I believe, why we should take a new look at these factors at this time and allow ourselves to respond to them. For today we are quite tangibly experiencing the power of chaos. We experience the primal, chaotic powers rising up from the very midst of a progressive society—which seems to know everything and be able to do anything—and attacking the very progress of which it is so proud. We see how, in the midst of prosperity, technological achievement and the scientific domination of the world, a nation can be destroyed from within; we see how the creation can be threatened by the chaotic powers which lurk in the depths of the human heart. We realize that neither money nor technology nor organizational ability alone can banish chaos. Only the real protective wall given to us by the Lord, the new family he has created for us, can do this. From this standpoint, it seems to me, this Passover celebration which has come down to us from the nomads, via Israel and through Christ, also has (in the deepest sense) an eminently political significance. We as a nation, we in Europe, need to go back to our spiritual roots, lest we become lost in self-destruction.

This feast needs to become a family celebration once again, for it is the family that is the real bastion of creation and humanity. Passover is a summons, urgently reminding us that the family is the living home in which humanity is nurtured, which banishes chaos and futility, and which must be protected as such. But we must add that the family can only be this sphere of humanity, this bastion of creation, if it is under the banner of the Lamb, if it is protected by the power of faith which comes from the love of Jesus Christ. The individual family cannot survive; it will disintegrate unless it is kept safe within the larger family which guarantees it and gives it security. So this night needs to be the night in which we set out once again on our twin paths: we set out on the path to the new city, the new family, the Church, and dedicate ourselves irrevocably to her, to our heart's true home; and then, on the basis of this family of Jesus Christ, we can proceed to grasp what is meant by the human family and by the humanity which sustains and protects us.

There is something else. Israel took over this festival from the cult and culture of the nomads. There it was the festival of spring, when they set off with their herds for new pastures. First of all, therefore, the tents were surrounded by a circle of lamb's blood. This was meant as a sign of defense against the power of death, which was encountered so frequently in the faceless desert. It explains why Israel still celebrated the day dressed in pilgrim clothes, as if ready to set off, and eating nomads' food: lamb, bitter herbs (in the place of salt) and unleavened bread. Thus Israel had brought these fundamental elements from its nomadic past into its rites of celebration. Passover was a continual reminder of the time when Israel itself was a people without a dwelling place, a wandering, homeless people. It told them again and again, "We are a wandering people, even now that we have a dwelling place; as human beings, we are never finally at home; ultimately nothing belongs to us, we are always on the move. And for that very reason, everything we have we share, and we belong to one another." In translating "Pasch" as "Passover", the ancient Church expressed Jesus Christ's passage through the zone of death into the new life of the Resurrection. For us too, therefore, Passover has become and remained a pilgrim feast. It also says to us, "We are only guests on earth, God's guests. We are only guests: the Lord, who himself became a guest and a wanderer, calls us to be open to all who have become homeless in this world. He summons us to be open to those who suffer, are forsaken, imprisoned, persecuted, for he is in them all." Israel's law, laid down for a people which had now become the resident possessor of the land, again and again exhibits protective clauses for those who are homeless, guests and wanderers. Again and again the message is hammered home to Israel: "Remember that you were a wanderer and a pilgrim!" We *are* wanderers and pilgrims. That is how we should understand the earth and our life; and we should treat each other accordingly. We are only guests on earth; we are pilgrims in the profoundest sense, that the earth is not ultimate, and we are on our way to the new world. The things of earth are not final and decisive. We hardly dare to say it any more, because people accuse us Christians of not having bothered about earthly matters, of having failed to build the new city in the world because we could always take refuge in the other world. But it is not true. The man who clasps the earth fast, who regards the earth as the only possible heaven, actually makes a hell of it, for he is trying to make it into something it cannot be. In trying to make it ultimate, he is setting himself against himself, against truth and against his fellowmen. No; it is only when we realize that we are wanderers that we become free from ultimate covetousness, free for one another. Only then can we be entrusted with the responsibility of fashioning the earth in such a way that, in the end, we shall be able to place it in God's hands. So let this Passover night, which reminds us of Jesus' final path, continually challenge us to bear in mind the final path we all must take and to remember that eventually we shall have to leave behind all our possessions. In the end it is not what we have that counts, but what we are. In the end we shall have to give an account of how, in this world and on the basis of our faith, we shared peace, a home and family with our fellow human beings, and how we helped to bring the new city to them.

Passover was celebrated at home. Jesus did this too. But after the meal he got up and went out, and he overstepped the bounds of the law by going beyond the Brook Kidron which marked the boundary of Jerusalem. He went out into the night. He did not fear the chaos, did not hide from it, but plunged into its deepest point, into the jaws of death: as we pray, he "descended into hell". He went out; that is to say, since the Church's rampart is faith and the love of Jesus Christ, the Church is not a bunker or a sealed fortress but an open city. Faith always means going out together with Jesus, not being afraid of the chaos, because he is the stronger one. He "went out" and we go out with him if we do the same. Faith means emerging from the walls to build places of faith and of love in the midst of the chaotic world by the power of Jesus Christ. The Lord "went out"—it is a sign of his power. He went out into the night of Gethsemane, the night of the Cross and the grave. He is the "stronger man" who stands up against the "strong man"—death— (Lk 11:21–23). The love of God—God's power—is stronger than the powers of destruction. So this very "going out", this setting out on the path of the Passion, when Jesus steps outside the boundary of the protective walls of the city, is a gesture of victory. The mystery of Gethsemane already holds within it the mystery of Easter joy. Jesus is the "stronger man". There is no power that can withstand him now; no place where he is not to be found. He summons us to dare to accompany him on his path; for where faith and love are, he is there, and the power of peace is there which overcomes nothingness and death.

At the end of the Holy Thursday liturgy we shall imitate the path taken by Jesus. We shall carry the Blessed Sacrament out of the cathedral and take it to the chapel of his loneliness and mortal anguish. We accompany him in the hour of his forsakenness, so that he is no longer forsaken. This Holy Thursday procession must not remain a mere liturgical gesture. It must be a commitment on our part to be continually entering into Jesus' forsakenness, to be continually seeking him, forgotten and derided, wherever he is lonely; to stand by him whenever men do not want to know him. Let us ask the Lord to let his light shine in all the dark places of this world, and to reveal it to us in times of loneliness and darkness. Let us ask him to be with us in the midst

of the darkness of this world and to use us to build
the new city, the place where his peace dwells, the
New Creation. Amen.

"The Lamb Redeemed the Sheep"
Reflections on the Symbolism of Easter

The lightness and joy which most of us associate with the idea of Easter do not alter the fact that the inner significance of this day is far harder for us to appreciate than, for instance, the meaning of Christmas. Birth, the child, the family—all this is part of our own experience. We are immediately attracted by the idea that God became a child, making little things great, rendering great things human, tangible and close to us. According to our faith, God has stepped into the world in the birth at Bethlehem, and this causes a ray of light to fall even on those who cannot accept the message as such.

In the case of Easter it is different. Here, God has not entered into our familiar life; on the contrary, he has broken through its limitations and entered a new realm beyond death. Here, he does not enter into our pattern of life but goes before us into a vast, unknown expanse, holding the torch aloft to encourage us to follow him. However, since we are only acquainted with things on this side of death, there is nothing in our experience we can link with these tidings. We have no ideas to come to the aid of the words; we are feeling our way blindly in unknown territory and are painfully aware of our short-sightedness and cramped footsteps.

It is thrilling, all the same, to learn, at least from the lips of someone who knows, of things that are of the greatest importance to all of us. Recent years have revealed a tremendous curiosity in the reports of people who have been clinically dead, who claim to have experienced what is beyond experience and seem to be able to speak of what lies behind the dark door of death. This inquisitiveness shows that the question of death is a burning topic to everyone. All these accounts leave us unsatisfied, however, because, after all, the people concerned were not really dead; they only underwent the special experience associated with a particular, extreme condition of human life and consciousness. No one can say whether their experience would have been confirmed had they been really dead. But he of whom Easter speaks—Jesus Christ—really "descended into hell". Jesus actually complied with the suggestion of the rich man: Let someone come back from the dead, and we will believe (Lk 16:27f.)! He, the true Lazarus, *did* come back so that we may believe. And do we? He did not come back with disclosures nor with exciting prospects of the "world beyond". But he did tell us that he is "going to prepare a place" for us (Jn 14:2–3). Is this surely not the most exciting news in the whole of history, though it is presented without any tickling of the senses?

Easter is concerned with something unimaginable. Initially the event of Easter comes to us solely through the word, not through the senses. So it is all the more important for us to be won over by the immensity of this word. Since, however, we can only think by employing sense images, the faith of the Church has always translated the Easter message into symbols which point to things that the word cannot express. The symbol of light (including the fire) plays a special part; the praise of the Paschal candle—a symbol of life in the midst of the darkened church—is actually a praise of him who proved victor over death. Thus the event of long ago is translated into our present time: where light conquers darkness, something of the Resurrection takes place. The consecration of water focuses on another element of creation, used as a symbol of the Resurrection: water can be a threat, a weapon of death. But the living spring water means fruitfulness, building oases of life in the middle of the desert. Then there is a third symbol of a very different kind: the sung Alleluia, the solemn singing of the Paschal liturgy, shows that the human voice, as well as crying, groaning, lamenting, speaking, can also sing. Moreover, the fact that man is able to summon the voices of creation and transform them into harmony—does this not give us a marvelous intimation of the transformations which we too, with creation, can undergo? Is it not a wonderful sign of that hope which enables us to anticipate what is to come and also to receive it here and now? Nor is the season at which Easter is celebrated a chance matter, either. Via the Jewish Passover, the Christian Easter has its roots far back in the history of religions, in the realm of the so-called natural religions. I am always struck by the emphasis Jesus places during his earthly journey on his "hour". He is going toward his death, but he avoids it until this hour has come (cf. Lk 13:31–35). In this way he quite deliberately links his mission with mankind's whole history of belief and with the signs to be found in creation. He ties the accomplishment of his mission to this particular feast and hence to the first full moon of spring. To those who only look at things from the point of view of technology or historicism, this must appear unintelligible and devoid of meaning. But Jesus thought otherwise. By linking his hour to the revolutions of the moon and the earth, to the cycles of nature, he situates his death in a cosmic context and, conversely, relates the cosmos to man. In the Church's great festivals the creation, too, joins in; or rather, in these festivals we enter into the rhythm of the earth and the heavenly bodies and hear the message they have to give. Thus nature's new morning that marks the first full moon of spring is also a sign belonging genuinely to the Easter message: creation speaks of us and to us. We can only understand ourselves, and Christ, properly, if we also learn how to listen to the voice of creation.

Today, however, I want to direct our attention to that symbol which was at the center of the Jewish Passover and thus naturally became the core of the Church's Easter symbolism, namely, the Paschal Lamb. It is remarkable how important a part is played in the Bible by the image of the lamb. We come across it in the very first pages, in the account of the sacrifice of Abel, the shepherd; and in the last book of Holy Scripture the Lamb is at the very center of heaven and earth. According to the Book of Revelation, the Lamb alone can open the seals of history. It is the Lamb, who appears as slain and yet lives, who receives the homage of all creatures in heaven and earth. The lamb which lets itself be killed without complaint is a symbol of meekness: Blessed are the meek, for they shall inherit the earth (Mt 5:5). The Lamb with his mortal wound tells us that, in the end, it is not those who kill who will be the victors; on the contrary, the world is sustained by those who sacrifice themselves. It is the sacrifice of him who becomes the "Lamb slain" that holds heaven and earth together. True victory lies in this sacrifice. It gives rise to that life which imparts a meaning to history, through all its atrocities, and which can finally turn them into a song of joy.

It is not through these passages, however, that I have come to realize the significance of the image of the lamb, but rather through that most puzzling story in the Bible, which continues to scandalize its readers and thus spurs us on to a deeper questioning about God and can lead us to a better understanding of his mystery. I refer to the story of the sacrifice of Isaac. As he climbs the mountain, he sees that there is no animal for the sacrifice. He asks his father about this and is told that "God will provide . . ." (Gen 22:8). Not until the very moment when Abraham lifts up his knife to slay Isaac do we grasp how truly he spoke: a ram is caught in a thicket and takes the place of Isaac as a sacrifice. Jewish thought continually returned to that mysterious moment when Isaac lay bound on the altar. Often enough, Israel was obliged to recognize its own situation in that of Isaac, bound and ready for the fatal knife, and was thus heartened to try to understand its own destiny. In Isaac, Israel had as it were meditated upon the truth of the word, "God will provide". Jewish tradition tells that, at the moment when Isaac uttered a cry of terror, the heavens opened and the boy saw the invisible mysteries of creation and the angelic choirs.[1] This is connected with another tradition according to which it was Isaac who created Israel's rite of worship; thus the Temple was built, not on Sinai, but on Moriah.[2] It is as though all worship originates in this glimpse on the part of Isaac—in what he then saw and afterward communicated. Finally, in this connection, there are various interpretations of the name Isaac, which contains

[1] E. Wiesel, *Adam oder das Geheimnis des Anfangs. Brüderliche Urgestalten* (Freiburg 1980), 93f. I am indebted to Wiesel for pointing out the remarkable article by K. Rohmann, "Das Lachen und die Hoffnung. Einige Erwägungen zur 'politischen Theologie' angesichts der 'Opferung Isaaks' (E. Wiesel)", in H. Waldenfels (ed.), *Theologie–Grund und Grenzen. Festgabe H. Dolch* (Paderborn 1982), 609–21.
[2] Rohmann, 618.

the root "laughter". First of all the Bible sees in the name an allusion to the sad, unbelieving laughter of Abraham and Sarah, who would not believe that they could still have a son (cf. Gen 17:17; 18:12). But once the promise comes true, it turns into joyful laughter; crabbed loneliness is dissolved in the joy of fulfillment (Gen 21:6). Later tradition refers the laughter no longer only to Isaac's parents but to Isaac himself.[3] And indeed, had he not grounds for laughter when the tension of mortal fear suddenly disappeared at the sight of the trapped ram, which solved the riddle? Did he not have cause to laugh when the sad and gruesome drama—the ascent of the mountain, his father binding him—suddenly had an almost comic conclusion, yet one that brought liberty and redemption? This was a moment in which it was shown that the history of the world is not a tragedy, the inescapable tragedy of opposing forces, but "divine comedy". The man who thought he had breathed his last was able to laugh.

Just as Jewish tradition continually returned to the story of Isaac, the Church Fathers also simply could not put this story down. They too asked what Isaac experienced at that final moment when he lay bound on the firewood. What did he see? Their answer is simpler and more realistic than that of the Jewish scholars. They say quite simply: he saw the ram which took his place and thus, at that moment, "redeemed" him. He saw the ram which thenceforward became the center of the Jewish cult as a whole. The Fathers, too, say that the Jewish cult ultimately aims to continue and to preserve the experience of that moment; it aims to achieve redemption by substitution. And they too are aware that Isaac,

---

[3] Rohmann, 618f.

on seeing the ram, had good reason for laughing; the sight of the ram gave him back the laughter he had so recently lost.

The Fathers go one step further, however. Isaac saw the ram: that is, he saw the sign of what was to come, of him who was to come as the Lamb. Seeing the lamb, he had caught sight of him who, for our sake, allowed himself to be caught in the thicket of history, who for our sake let himself be bound, who took our place and is our redemption. To that extent, according to the Fathers, Isaac *did* actually have a glimpse of heaven. His sight of this ram *was* a view of heaven opened. For in it he saw the God who provides and who stands waiting on the very threshold of death. In seeing the ram he saw the God who not only provides but provides himself in becoming the Lamb, so that man may become man and may live. When Isaac caught sight of the ram in this last moment, he saw exactly what, on Patmos, John saw in the opened heavens. John describes it thus: "And between the throne and the four living creatures and among the elders, I saw a Lamb standing, as though it had been slain. . . . And I heard every creature in heaven and on earth and under the earth and in the sea, and all therein, saying, 'To him who sits upon the throne and to the Lamb be blessing and honor and glory and might for ever and ever!' " (Rev 5:6, 13). Isaac's sight of the lamb showed him what cult is: God himself provides his cult, through which he releases and redeems man, and gives him back the laughter of joy which becomes creation's hymn of praise.

Now you might say, what concern of ours are the Church Fathers and Jewish stories? Well, I do not think it is difficult to see that the Isaac of whom we are speaking is we ourselves. We climb up the mountain of time, bearing with us the instruments of our own death. At first the goal is far distant. We do not think of it; the present is enough: the morning on the mountain, the song of the birds, the sun's brightness. We feel we do not need to know about our destination, since the way itself is enough. But the longer it grows, the more unavoidable the question becomes: Where is it going? What does it all mean? We look with apprehension at the signs of death which, up to now, we had not noticed, and the fear rises within us that perhaps the whole of life is only a variation of death; that we have been deceived, and that life is actually not a gift at all but an imposition. Then the strange reply, "God will provide", sounds more like an excuse than an explanation. Where this view predominates, where talk of "God" is no longer believable, humor dies. In such a case man has nothing to laugh about anymore; all that is left is a cruel sarcasm or that rage against God and the world with which we are all acquainted. But the person who has seen the Lamb— Christ on the Cross—knows that God *has* provided. The heavens are not opened, none of us has seen the "invisible mysteries of creation and the angelic choirs". All we can see is—like Isaac—the Lamb, of whom the Apostle Peter says that he was destined before the foundation of the world (1 Pet 1:20). But this sight of the Lamb—the crucified Christ—is in fact our glimpse of heaven, of what God has eternally provided for us. In this Lamb we actually do glimpse heaven, and we see God's gentleness, which is neither indifference nor weakness but power of the highest order. It is in this way, and only thus, that we see the mysteries of creation and catch a little of the song of the angels—indeed, we can try to join with them, somewhat, in singing the Alleluia of Easter Day. Since we see the Lamb, we can laugh and give thanks; we too see from him what worship is.

Let us come back to the Church Fathers. As we have seen, they discerned, in the lamb, an anticipation of Jesus. Moreover, they say that Jesus is both the lamb and Isaac.[4] He is the lamb who allowed himself to be caught, bound and slain. He is also Isaac, who looked into heaven; indeed, where Isaac only saw signs and symbols, Jesus actually entered heaven, and since that time the barrier between God and man is broken down. Jesus is Isaac, who, risen from the dead, comes down from the mountain with the laughter of joy in his face. All the words of the Risen One manifest this joy—this laughter of redemption: if you see what I see and have seen, if you catch a glimpse of the whole picture, you will laugh! (cf. Jn 16:20). In the Baroque period the liturgy used to include the *risus paschalis*, the Easter laughter. The Easter homily had to contain a story which made people laugh, so that the church resounded with a joyful laughter.[5] That may be a somewhat superficial form of Christian joy. But is there not something very beautiful and appro-

---

[4] Origen, *In Genesim Hom* 8, 6–9 PG 12:206–9. This is a fundamental text; its lines of thought are developed in Origen's followers, e.g., Gregory of Nyssa, *In Christi resurr. hom.* 1 PG 46:601 C, which also asserts that Isaac—prefiguring Christ—was both the heir and the lamb. Even before Origen, the theme had been proposed: cf. Meliton of Sardis' fragments on Genesis in PG 5:1216 B–1217 A. The theme of the lamb is broadly set forth, in the context of the Passover lamb, in the Passover homily; nos. 59 and 69, however, also take up the Isaac story. On this, cf. J. Blank, *Vom Passa. Die älteste christliche Osterpredigt* (Freiburg 1963), 72, 76. The christological perspective of the story of Abel is also presupposed by the "Supra quae" prayer of the Roman Canon, cf. J. A. Jungmann, *The Mass of the Roman Rite II* (1955), 228ff.; T. Schnitzler, *Die Messe in der Betrachtung I* (Freiburg 1955), 95. A helpful introduction to the significance of the image of the lamb in Christian art can be found in H. and M. Schmidt, *Die vergessene Bildersprache der christlichen Kunst* (Munich 1981), 72–78.

[5] Examples are to be found in G. Lohmeier (ed.), *Geistliches Donnerwetter. Bayerische Barockpredigten* (dtv 1967).

priate about laughter becoming a liturgical symbol? And isn't it a tonic when we still hear, in the play of cherub and ornament in baroque churches, that laughter which testified to the freedom of the redeemed? Surely it is a sign of an Easter faith when Haydn remarked, concerning his church compositions, that he felt a particular joy when thinking of God: "As I came to utter the words of supplication, I could not suppress my joy but loosed the reins of my elated spirits and wrote 'allegro' over the Miserere, etc."?

The Book of Revelation's vision of heaven expresses what we see by faith at Easter: the Lamb who was slain lives. Since he lives, our weeping comes to an end and is transformed into laughter (cf. Rev 5:4f.). When we look at the Lamb we see heaven opened. God sees us, and God acts, albeit differently from the way we think and would like him to act. Only since Easter can we really utter the first article of faith; only on the basis of Easter is this profession rich and full of consolation: I believe in God, the Father Almighty. For it is only from the Lamb that we know that God is really Father, really Almighty. No one who has grasped that can ever be utterly despondent and despairing again. No one who has grasped that will ever succumb to the temptation to side with those who kill the Lamb. No one who has understood this will know ultimate fear, even if he gets into the situation of the Lamb. For there he is in the safest possible place.

Easter, therefore, invites us not only to listen to Jesus but also, as we do so, to develop our interior sight. This greatest festival of the Church's year encourages us, by looking at him who was slain and is risen, to discover the place where heaven is opened. If we comprehend the message of the Resurrection, we recognize that heaven is not completely sealed off above the earth. Then—gently and yet with immense power—something of the light of God penetrates our life. Then we shall feel the surge of joy for which, otherwise, we wait in vain. Everyone who is penetrated by something of this joy can be, in his own way, a window through which heaven can look upon earth and visit it. In this way, what Revelation foresees can come about: every creature in heaven and on earth and under the earth and in the sea, everything in the world, is filled with the joy of the redeemed (cf. Rev 5:13). To the extent that we realize this, the words of the departing Jesus—who, parting from us, is the coming Jesus—are fulfilled: "Your sorrow will turn into joy" (Jn 16:20). And, like Sarah, people who share an Easter faith can say: "God has made me laugh; every one who hears will laugh with me" (Gen 21:6).

Christ the Liberator

An Easter Homily

The Eastern Church's picture of Easter has taken a different path from that of the Western world and the images which are familiar to us. She does not show the Lord having burst from the grave, suspended in a brilliant, divine glory above the world, as in Grünewald's impressive and masterful painting. Since Scripture itself does not portray the Resurrection event, Eastern believers too refrained from depicting it. The icon, by contrast, represents as it were the mysterious inner dimension of the event of Easter which is indicated by a few words of Scripture and which we profess in the Creed when we say, "He descended into hell". In the perspective of the icon, this is an affirmation concerning Jesus' victory. The icon shows him having shattered the bolt of this world, having torn its gates from their hinges. It depicts him as the "stronger man" who has opened and penetrated the domain of the "strong man". It portrays him as the Victor, having burst through the supposedly impregnable fortress of death, such that death is now no longer a place of no return; its doors lie open. Christ, in the aura of his wounded love, stands in this doorway, addresses the still somnolent Adam and takes him by the hand to lead him forth. The liturgy of Holy Saturday circles around this event.[1]

---

[1] Cf. the convincing remarks of P. Evdokimov, *L'Art de l'icône. Théologie de la beauté* (Desclée 1970), 265–75.

In an ancient Easter Vigil homily, ascribed to Epiphanius, which is also read in our liturgy now, we hear what we may imagine to be the words of Jesus Christ.[2] He says to Adam, "I am your God, yet I have become your son. I am in you, and you are in me. We together are a single, indivisible person." Thus it is clear that this Adam does not signify an individual in a dim and distant past: the Adam addressed by the victorious Christ is we ourselves—"I am in you, and you are in me". Having taken human nature, he is now present in human flesh, and we are present in him, the Son. Epiphanius quotes and expands a passage from the Letter to the Ephesians: "Awake, O sleeper, and arise from the dead, and Christ shall give you light. I have not created you to be in prison forever. I did not make you for the dungeon."[3] This pronouncement contains the whole Christian message of Easter. Again, we see that this prison which Christ opens is not somewhere or other in the unknown depths of the earth. It can be anywhere—in the prisons of this world but also in the midst of luxury and apparent freedom. A theologian of the ancient Church once wrote, "Christ descended into hell when he spoke with Caiaphas."[4] What a terrible dictum! But how many Caiaphases are there in the world? How much of Caiaphas is there in each of us? Truly, the prison which alienates us from ourselves can be anywhere and everywhere. What then makes this prison, this alienation,

[2] PG 43:440–64; cf. Evdokimov, 270. On the textual history of the Homily, cf. *Clavis Patrum Graecorum II* (1974), no. 3768; cf. also J. Quasten, *Patrology* 3 (Utrecht 1960): 395.

[3] Eph 5:14; Ps.-Epiphanius (see note 2 above).

[4] A. Grillmeier cites this dictum of a Syrian Monophysite in *TheolPhil* 55 (1980): 589. The original reference is in A. de Halleux, *Philoxène de Mabbog* (Louvain 1963).

which robs man of freedom and against which he rebels in a thousand different ways? What makes man a prisoner, incapable of being himself?

What is the specific characteristic of a prison? On reflection, it is surely the deprivation of freedom, and, at a deeper level, it is that the human being is denied communication, i.e., normal fellowship and relationship with others, along with normal participation in activity in the world. I am reminded of the phrase in which the Bishops' Conference in Puebla summed up their strategy of liberation: *comunión y participación*—fellowship and participation. These two give substance to man. Where both are cut off, his own selfhood is denied him. Yet if we see our freedom solely in these two elements, fellowship and participation, we shall be forgetting a third fundamental element, which is actually the first, the basis for all real freedom, without which man can never genuinely discover his dignity and his freedom. This third element is mentioned in the words of Ephesians we have just heard: "Awake . . . and Christ shall give you light." In ancient times the really terrible thing about prisons was that they cut people off from the light of day and plunged them into darkness. So at a deeper level, the real alienation, unfreedom and imprisonment of man consists in his want of truth. If he does not know truth, if he does not know who he is, why he is there and what the reality of this world consists in, he is only stumbling around in the dark. He is a prisoner, he is not "being's freedman". The first and most fundamental of all human rights is the right to God, the Holy Father said on his visit to Ireland. Without this basic right, which is also the right to truth, the other human rights are not enough. Without this fundamental right to truth and to God, man becomes degraded to the level of a mere creature of needs. And the deep darkness and alienation of our times is shown in the fact that we have powers and abilities but do not know what they are for; we have so much knowledge that we are no longer able to believe and see truth; we are no longer able to embrace the totality. Our philosophy is that of Pilate: What is truth? This only looks like a question: in fact it is a statement, to the effect that there is no truth, and only idiots and fanatics imagine they have it or argue about it. But if this is how things are, if man has no truth, only abilities, he is fundamentally alienated, and "participation" is only an empty play-acting in the dark, deluding man with the notion of freedom and hurting him deeply. There is nothing for-tuitous about the strident protests against such empty freedom: man, deprived of truth, has been dishonored.

"I did not make you for the dungeon. Arise, and Christ shall give you light!" The ancient Church used these words of Christ to Adam as a baptismal hymn, as the believing Church's summons to the candidate. Thus it expresses the fact that Easter, the victory in which Jesus Christ breaks down the walls of alienation and leads us out into the open air, is to be heard continually in the sacrament of baptism. In this sacrament he takes us by the hand; in it, Truth speaks to us and shows us to the way to freedom. Wherever baptism is celebrated, the reality of Easter takes place here and now. So the annual feast of Easter is an invitation to us to return to our own baptism, to seize the hand of Truth which reaches out to lead us to the light. To renew our baptism, and hence genuinely to celebrate Easter, the feast of liberation, means that we renew our acceptance of the truth of faith; it means entering into the light of this truth and, as believers, overcoming the darkness of truth's absence. In this way we discover the real core of our freedom.

"Arise, Christ shall give you light!" The Church's real ministry of liberation is to hold aloft the flame of truth in the world. Liberation is our continual and fresh acceptance of truth as the path of life set before us.

We must acknowledge, however, that faith is seriously weakened and threatened within the Church. Even we in the Church have lost courage. We feel it to be arrogance or triumphalism to assume that the Christian faith tells us the truth. We have picked up the idea that all religions are the product of history, some developing this way and others that, and that every person is as he is because of the accident of birth. Such a view reduces religion from the level of truth to the level of habit. It becomes an empty flux of inherited traditions which no longer have any significance. But this view also eliminates a crucial affirmation from the Christian faith, namely, Christ's "I am the Truth"—and hence the Way, hence also the Life. There is a great temptation to say, "But there is so much suffering in the world!—let's suspend the question of truth for a while. First let's get on with the great social tasks of liberation; then, one day, we will indulge in the luxury of the question of truth." In fact, however, if we postpone the question of truth and declare it to be unimportant, we are emasculating man, depriving him of the very core of his human dignity. If there is no truth, everything is a matter of indifference. Then social order swiftly becomes compulsion, and participation becomes violation. The Church's real contribution to liberation, which she can never postpone and which is most urgent today, is to proclaim truth in the world, to affirm that God is, that God knows us, and that God is as Jesus Christ has revealed him, and that, in Jesus Christ, he has given us the path of life. Only then can there be such a thing as conscience, man's receptivity for truth, which

127

gives each person direct access to God and makes him greater than every imaginable world system.

"I did not make you for the dungeon." In this Easter hour let us ask the Lord to visit the dungeons of this world; all the prisons which are hushed up by a propaganda which knows no truth, by a strategy of disinformation, keeping us in the dark and constituting our dungeon. Let us ask him to enter into the spiritual prisons of this age, into the darkness of our lack of truth, revealing himself as the Victor who tears down the gates and says to us, "I, your God, have become your Son. Come out! I have not created you to be in prison for ever. I did not make you for the dungeon." In his play *No Exit* Jean Paul Sartre portrays man as a being who is hopelessly trapped. He sums up his gloomy picture of man in the words, "Hell is other people". This being so, hell is everywhere, and there is no exit, the doors are everywhere closed.

Christ, however, says to us, "I, your God, have become your Son. Come out!" Now the exact opposite is true: heaven is other people. Christ summons us to find heaven in him, to discover him in others and thus to be heaven to each other. He calls us to let heaven shine into this world, to build heaven here. Jesus stretches out his hand to us in his Easter message, in the mystery of the sacraments, so that Easter may be *now*, so that the light of heaven may shine forth in this world and the doors may be opened. Let us take his hand! Amen.